A CENTURY OF STYLE

TEXT AND PHOTOGRAPHY BY HENRY RASMUSSEN

IMPERIAL PALACE AUTO COLLECTION, LAS VEGAS, NEVADA

PUBLISHED BY MOTORBOOKS INTERNATIONAL

First published in 1990 by Motorbooks International,

729 Prospect Avenue, Osceola, WI 54020, USA.

Printed in Hong Kong.

A CENTURY OF STYLE has been published with the full cooperation of the
Imperial Palace Auto Collection, 3535 Las Vegas Boulevard South,
Las Vegas, NV 89109, USA.

Library of Congress Cataloging-in-Publication Data

ISBN 0-87938-462-X

Photography and design by Henry Rasmussen.

Text by Henry Rasmussen; additional text by Lowell C. Paddock.

Project editorial services by Paddock & Pearson, Inc.

CREDITS

■ The work contained within these covers results from several people without whose skill and dedication it could never have been accomplished. ■ The first phase, the location photography, was undertaken with the assistance of John Workman and Frank Borelli, both of the Collection staff, who were responsible for the transportation of the cars as well as their detailing. John and Frank also assisted with the studio photography, where their proficiency in rigging lights and reflectors soon rivaled that of experienced professionals. ■ The crucial job of printing the black-and-white photographs was the responsibility of Theresa Holmes of Las Vegas, whose ability to transfer my photographic intentions to paper proved exceptional. ■ For assistance with the research and writing I called on the lexical talents of Lowell Paddock, of Paddock & Pearson, Inc., in Venice, California, who, as copy editor and fact checker, had a profound influence on the text. Augmenting him with this task was his equally able partner, Stephen Pearson, who made sure that everything arrived and departed on schedule. Assisting with the research were Randy Ema, Terry Dunham, Strother MacMinn and Dennis Adler. ■ During the graphic design phase of the book, Bob Lee of Bob Lee Graphics in Los Angeles, California, operated his desktop publishing system so efficiently that all the loose ends came together very smoothly. ■ In addition to those

mentioned above, I am indebted to Stacy Best, Eulogio Cacicedo, Gaynell Lapinski, Hagan Stewart and Vicki Turngren, all on the Collection staff. ■ Further assistance was provided by the Beringer, Clos Pegase, Freemark Abbey and Inglenook wineries, all of Napa Valley, California, who made their respective properties available for location photography, as did the Landmark and Glass Pool Hotels, both of Las Vegas, the Valley of Fire State Park, Nevada, and the San Diego Port Authority, California. ■ The Behring, Harrah and Al Michaelian collections each made their archives available for research and permitted use of their historic photographs, as did Road & Track magazine. ■ The color separations, printing and binding were supplied by Bookbuilders Limited of Kowloon Bay, Hong Kong through the publisher's production office in Stillwater, Minnesota. ■ Overseeing the entire project as its producer was Motorbooks International Publisher Tim Parker, whose seasoned experience guided the project from its commencement to its conclusion. ■ Last, but not least, I am truly indebted to Ralph Engelstad and Richie Clyne, owner and administrator, respectively, of the Collection, without whose involvement this book would never have become a reality.

Henry Rasmussen, March 1990

CONTENTS

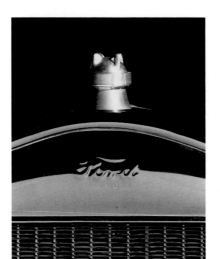

INTRODUCTION

■ When I bought my first car in 1949, at the age of nineteen, I obviously had no inkling that one day I would own more automobiles than I could keep track of. The thought that I, thirty years down the road, would build a museum to display a portion of my cars, and that it would take half a dozen warehouses to store the rest, would have seemed preposterous to me at the time. ■ That first automobile, a 1939 Ford two-door sedan, was not an object that I cherished for its mechanical sophistication—that part of the car was probably not overly impressive, anyway. As a matter of fact, I spent very little time under its hood; between school and work—I've had a steady job since I was thirteen—there was simply no time. ■ Among other automobiles that I remember well was the one my wife Betty—she has been by my side since 1954—and I owned when we were married, a 1951 Pontiac two-door sedan. It seems the car people drive as newlyweds is the one they most often recall with nostalgia—that and the first car they ever drove. ■ I'm not sure why I favored Pontiac in those days. Perhaps it was because my father—a man I admired immensely—always drove Pontiacs. Or perhaps it was simply because of that catchy slogan, "Dollar for dollar, you can't beat a Pontiac." ■ My many years in the construction business made me appreciate the versatility of the pickup truck, and I have owned and

enjoyed a great number of them. One of those workhorses was a 1949 Chevrolet 3/4-ton. I have had it restored, and, as a reminder of my roots, it's displayed in the Collection alongside Packards and Duesenbergs. ■ People often ask me how I got the idea for the Collection. It was actually a thought that ripened over a period of time. It seems that, as I myself matured, I became more and more attracted to things of the past. The fact that I finally found myself with the means to collect them was no doubt an important reason. ■ The automobile has played a pivotal role in the development of society as we know it, and today it touches the lives of every individual. All, regardless of age, sex and education, seem to have a soft spot for the automobile, be it new or old. This fascination is illustrated by the fact that more than 400,000 people visit the Collection every year. ■ It gives me great satisfaction to share the intrigue of the automobile with so many. The thought of sharing was also the driving force behind the publication of this book, which will no doubt widen the Collection's audience even further. ■ As you browse through these pages, remember that there is more where this came from, so please stop by next time you visit Las Vegas.

Ralph Engelstad, owner,
Imperial Palace Hotel, Las Vegas, Nevada.

PART ONE

THE COLLECTION

■ The Imperial Palace employs the latest in visual communications technology to promote the Collection's virtues. The photo sequence below captures one of three 700-square-foot electronic message boards strategically located on the facades of the hotel so as to catch the attention of the ever-flowing foot and wheel traffic that travels the Strip. Their 25,000 multicolored light bulbs—drawing electricity at the rate of 300 amps each—illuminate the Las Vegas skyline day and night.

■ The initial steps on the road that led to the formation of Imperial Palace Auto Collection, as with all beginnings, were modest ones. The tentative nature of these early efforts are illustrated by the fact that when Ralph Engelstad bought his first collector car, a 1929 Ford Model A Roadster, the motivations guiding his purchase—as well as the intended focus of the museum he planned to build—were completely different from those that directed the building of the Collection as it stands today. ■ Consistent with Engelstad's vision, that first Ford, purchased in March 1979 and pictured with Engelstad on page 8, was meant to form the nucleus of an exhibit featuring Fords exclusively. His plan called for the acquisition of one example of every model and year produced by the manufacturer, some 241 automobiles in all, according to Engelstad's calculations. ■ For a long time, however, the lone Ford constituted the entire range of the Collection. With Engelstad's time occupied organizing the expansion of the hotel and casino, plans for the museum had to take a back seat, and Engelstad didn't get around to buying his second Ford until November 1980. ■ From then on, however, Engelstad devoted more time to the museum project and soon became a familiar sight at collector car auctions around the country. Additional Fords soon joined the initial two, among them a 1919 Model T, a 1928 Model A depot hack

■ With five twenty-story towers—one of which forms the backdrop in the photograph

below—and a total of 2700 rooms, the Imperial Palace is the largest privately owned hotel in the world. As such, it is in

a unique position to draw visitors to the Collection. No less than 400,000 tour the 65,000-square-foot

facility each year, making it one of the world's most popular automotive museums. The 1936 Mercedes-Benz

Spezial-Roadster pictured here has come to represent the spirit of the Collection.

■ *These scenes, featuring some of the Collection's many dioramas, were photographed at night
when visitors would not obscure them. The ghostly darkness is given further drama by costumed mannequins, who at
times seem to come alive. Below, one area of the Collection features a farm scene, with a 1919 Ford
Model T delivery truck as its main attraction. A number of cars are displayed with their hoods open; at the top
of the page, a 1937 Cord 812 and a 1957 Thunderbird show off their potent engines.*

and a 1966 Mustang GT Convertible. ■ It was on the auction circuit that Engelstad met Richie Clyne, who at the time operated his own collector car dealership. The chance encounter proved to be pivotal since, at Clyne's urging, the theme of the planned museum was expanded to represent a selection of all types and makes of cars—although the primary focus would be on American automobiles, with a particular emphasis on such exclusive bodystyles as town cars and limousines. ■ Empowered with Engelstad's commission, Clyne proceeded to peruse auctions and private collections across the nation and around the world for suitable acquisitions for the Collection. What had been initiated on a small scale soon assumed major proportion as cars began arriving in Las Vegas at a breakneck pace. ■ Some of the Collection's most distinctive examples of the pioneer era were added at this time, including such historic treasures as the 1897 Duryea and the 1897 Haynes-Apperson. Further acquisitions during this initial period spanned an intriguing range, exemplified by such selections as an exquisitely rare 1941 Lincoln Touring Car, a one-off chariot of comfort and style built for Mrs. Henry Ford, as well as a Lilliputian 1962 Nash Metropolitan, a most lovable expression of automotive ingenuity. ■ Given the swelling assortment of cars accumulating in various Las Vegas warehouses, the need for a perma-

■ *In the illustration at the bottom of the previous page, Henry Ford himself is seen pondering*

the underhood simplicity of his Model T, its four-cylinder engine in this case providing motive power for a 1917 tanker truck.

The large illustration on this page recreates a scene from the fairy-tale life of the King of Siam, whose

1928 Delage occupies the center stage. Many displays have colorful murals painted on the wall behind them,

depicting scenes relating to the automobile they accompany.

■ Below, two of the numerous military vehicles contained in the Collection. The image of power and simplicity presented by the front end of a 1940 Dodge Command Car is indicative of the strength that helped America win World War II. At the top of the page, a curious vehicle from the other side, the German Kettenrad, a small, track-type personnel carrier. Other military exhibits range from a German Krausse Maffei—the largest personnel carrier ever built—to an American paratrooper's lightweight bicycle.

nent home for the Collection became increasingly urgent. Engelstad's plan for such a facility called for the top floor of the five-story Imperial Palace parking structure to be enclosed, creating a 65,000-square-foot area that would allow the exhibition of approximately 200 cars. ■ The grand opening of the Imperial Palace Auto Collection took place on the last day of November 1981, in a festive celebration attended by local dignitaries that culminated in Engelstad's wielding scissors to cut the traditional ribbon. ■ The man whose ambition had made the Collection a reality, Ralph Engelstad, was born in Thief River Falls, Minnesota, in 1930. One day in 1948, when Engelstad, fresh out of high school, labored at his part-time job unloading boxcars in Grand Forks, a co-worker—who happened to be a university professor—encouraged him to attend college, an eventuality that until then had not been included in the young man's still-diffuse master plan for his life. A hockey scholarship—Engelstad was already an accomplished goalie—made the college option a reality. ■ At one point tempted by an offer to join the Chicago Blackhawks as a professional player, Engelstad instead opted for the more prudent choice of starting his own construction company, a move made possible thanks to a $2500 loan from Valley Bank of Grand Forks, North Dakota, a local bank with a nose for budding potential. ■ In the

■ *Pictured here is that portion of the Collection devoted to fire apparatus. Its centerpiece is a massive*

1913 Seagrave pumper, which is joined by a 1915 Ford LaFrance ladder truck. At the bottom of the previous page is a

1927 Harley-Davidson, one of a number of motorcycles on display. Additional two-wheelers include a rare

1908 Experiment, a quartet of handsome Pierce-Arrows, a handful of Indians—among them the 1947 model once

owned by actor Steve McQueen—and a 1955 Ariel, the British thoroughbred.

■ With its inventory of vehicles exceeding 600—and still growing—the Collection is forced to house many of its automobiles in auxiliary storage areas prior to their restoration or display. Seen on these pages are glimpses of the Rolls-Royce and Mercedes-Benz holdings—two of the largest concentrations of these marques in the world. The Rolls-Royces, which currently number more than fifty, are mostly American-built. Among these, a 1930 Phantom I "Beetleback" by Brewster stands out as one of the finest.

course of the next decade—a portion of which he still spent in school—Engelstad went from erecting farm storage buildings for the State of North Dakota to building complete housing projects. The young entrepreneur invested his earnings in land and apartment complexes, but when, in the late Fifties, the bottom fell out of the local economy, he sold his holdings and moved west to booming Las Vegas. ■ During the next half-dozen years, Engelstad erected tract housing in Las Vegas as well as numerous commercial buildings at the Nevada Test Site. In 1965, he bought the Thunderbird Air Field, only to turn around and sell it to Howard Hughes two years later—a deal that facilitated an expansion to the famed Strip, although at its out-of-the-mainstream south end, where Engelstad bought the 116-room Kona Kai, later to become the Klondike. From his new vantage point, Engelstad appraised a move to a more advantageous spot on the Strip. The opportunity finally presented itself in 1971, when the 176-room Flamingo Capri—strategically located opposite Caesar's Palace—came on the market. ■ Engelstad soon discovered that, due to the disproportionately high value of the land, earnings from the hotel operation hardly paid its property taxes—prompting a choice between selling or building. With construction being Engelstad's primary business, his choice of the latter seemed obvious. Today, follow-

■ In the scene below, a 1936 Mercedes-Benz 500K Spezial-Roadster divides two rows of Mercedes-Benz

and Rolls-Royce automobiles. The Spezial-Roadster, with its stunning combination of beauty and performance, was one of

the most breathtaking bodystyles to emerge from any European automaker or coachbuilder during the late Thirties.

Another Daimler-Benz milestone of the period was the monumental 770K, of which the Collection owns a large number,

a few of which are lined up here form a backdrop to the Spezial-Roadster.

■ Illustrated on this page is the Collection's restoration shop, a 25,000-square-foot facility encompassing separate areas for bodywork, upholstery repair and mechanical repair. Below, dramatic stage illumination raises the highlights of a partially restored Mercedes-Benz 770K. Its gleaming engine stands finished, while its chassis awaits the completion of the fenders and hood. A number of demanding, ground-up restorations have been executed here, the Collection's Mercedes-Benz G4 among the most difficult.

ing a succession of expansions, the Imperial Palace and its five towers can accommodate as many as 5300 guests—a capacity that currently ranks it as the eighth largest hotel in the world. Through it all, Engelstad has held on to his sole ownership of the huge complex, allowing him to follow a course of independence; Imperial Palace remains the only privately owned major hotel on the Las Vegas strip. ■ Richie Clyne, the Collection's administrator since its inception shared his boss's appetite for Fords. In Clyne's case, it all began with a 1930 Model A he bought as a twelve-year old living on New York's Long Island. ■ Clyne's interest in vintage machinery eventually led him to a career in auto mechanics. He still could not get enough of automobiles, however, and began restoring collector cars in his spare time. The hobby soon led to a pattern of buying and selling, and ultimately to a successful business enterprise. ■ Once in Engelstad's employ, Clyne spearheaded many a dramatic effort to obtain cars for the Collection, among them the purchase of Hollywood's venerable Pacific Auto Rental, a deal that involved obtaining the entire company and its stable of 128 cars, just to get to one automobile—the extremely rare 1938 Mercedes-Benz G4 Geländewagen. ■ Another venture led Clyne to the doorsteps of W. C. Fields' mistress, actress Carlotta Monti, who, following the famous comedian's death in

■ At the bottom of the page, far left, one of the Collection's craftsmen takes the rough edges off one fender, while in the picture to the right, a second craftsman wet sands another prior to painting in order to eliminate any imperfections. At the top of the page is an assortment of restored gauges and lights; to the right, a still-life is composed from spare Mercedes-Benz radiator shells. A warehouse alongside the Collection's restoration shop holds thousands of parts—everything from hood ornaments to complete engines.

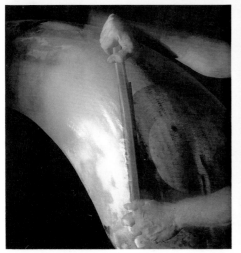

■ The Imperial Palace functions as host to "The Auction," an annual event run jointly by

Richie Clyne and Don Williams, administrators of, respectively, the Imperial Palace and the Behring Museum of Blackhawk,

California. Originally organized to facilitate the sale of surplus cars from the two museums, the event

soon attracted sellers—as well as buyers—from all across the country and around the world. The special allure

of the annual event is its "no reserve" policy, which assures the sale of every entry.

1949, was left with nothing but his 1938 Cadillac V-16—a treasure she had sentimentally maintained in a small garage behind her rented apartment. Repeated wooing by Clyne could not convince Monti to part with the car, until Clyne finally worked out a package deal that included the promise that mannequins of Fields and Monti would be displayed with the car. ■ In recent years the Collection has changed direction once again as the targets for acquisition have become the absolute cream of the automotive crop— today, it encompasses one of the world's largest concentrations of Duesenbergs, American Rolls-Royces and late-Thirties Mercedes-Benzes. Many of these treasured examples of automotive history have been painstakingly resurrected in the Collection's own fully equipped, 25,000-square-foot restoration facility which includes individual departments devoted to paint, bodywork, upholstery repair and mechanical restoration. ■ One of the world's ten best automotive museums, the Imperial Palace Auto Collection now features over 600 cars and continues to grow as the selection is refined and expanded. With the passing of nearly three million visitors down its aisles to date, the Collection is also one of the world's most popular, and, as such, stands as a tribute to the man whose dream it represents, but more profoundly, as a monument to the creative passions that gave the world the automobile.

■ Billed as "The Sale of the Century," the two-day event indeed lives up to its appellation.

Limited to 500 automobiles, The Auction is attended by some 3000 registered bidders, arriving from such far corners of

the world as Hong Kong and Johannesburg. The elite automobiles that have passed across the block

at record-breaking prices include one of the six Bugatti Royales—its unforgettable visage seen in the picture at

the bottom left—which reached the $11,000,000 mark in the 1989 auction.

PART TWO

THE DETAILS

■ *The following ten pages focus on the details that make up the whole of an automobile*

—elements that present both visual beauty and technical interest. Displayed on this page are the faces of some of the

most unique and trendsetting automobiles ever created. Below, the novel horseshoe shape of the Bugatti

radiator has been its trademark since Ettore Bugatti began building cars in 1909. Here, the radiator of a 1937 Type 57

reflects subtle design changes introduced by Ettore's talented son, Jean.

■ *Four masterpieces of the art of steel sculpture are represented in the illustrations on this page.*

Top left, the 1948 Tucker by Alex Tremulis. Next to it, Gordon Buehrig's 1937 Cord 812, whose retractable headlights

were an automotive first and an essential part of the look that made this Cord one of the all-time styling

greats. At the bottom of the page, Phil Wright's 1933 Pierce-Arrow Silver Arrow. To the right, the curvaceous

extravagance of Harley Earl, as expressed by the 1957 Cadillac.

■ *Speed and flight were among the favorite themes of many classic hood ornaments.*

At the top of this page is Buick's Mercury, cast in a variety of configurations by Ternstedt of Detroit. Below it, Packard's

"Goddess of Speed" took its cue from a similar design Bazin created for Isotta Fraschini. To the right, the

"Spirit of the Wind" decorates a 1939 Packard radiator. This design was created by Réné Lalique, France's famous

glass and jewelry maker, and can be illuminated by a bulb located in its base.

■ Rolls-Royce's "Spirit of Ecstasy" came in a variety of sizes and metals. At first fitted sporadically, the mascot became a catalog item in 1921. In the early days, sculptor Sykes put the finishing touches to each copy, giving them a special individuality. The metals he specified corresponded roughly to the ones used in the radiators themselves, polished bronze when radiators were made from bronze, nickel-plating in the days of nickel, and chrome-plating when radiators were built from stainless steel.

■ This photograph of the dashboard from the Collection's 1916 Simplex highlights the
exquisite craftsmanship that characterized the era in general and this car in particular. Its nautical theme, notable in a
number of exterior details, was carried through to the interior, where a smoothly crafted railing curves
around the entire cockpit. Having been cosseted by connoisseurs all its life—as indicated by its 1947 Glidden
Tour badge—the Simplex is completely original, down to its eight-day Waltham clock.

■ At right, the instruments from the Collection's 1933 Pierce-Arrow Silver Arrow are tastefully but logically grouped in a tight cluster. At the bottom of the page, the speedometer and clock mounted in the rear compartment of a 1931 Cadillac V-16 dual-cowl phaeton kept passengers informed of time and motion. Pictured to the left are the steering wheel and instrument cluster of the 1948 Tucker, which, in keeping with its advanced design theme, were a radical departure from the designs of the classic era.

■ An even dozen was the perfect number of wooden spokes on Renault's 1923 artillery-type
wheel, seen in the illustration below. The hub carried no decoration—just a simple "Automobiles Renault" spelled out in a
circle. By 1939, spoked wheels, both wood and metal, had been supplemented by pressed-steel wheels
topped by hubcaps as seen below, right, on a Cadillac V-16. Its super-wide white sidewalls provide a commanding
yet delicate counterpoint for the V-16 logo at the center of the wheel.

■ Fifty-six tempered steel spokes support the hub of this Rolls-Royce wheel. The automobile

shown in this photograph is a 1928 Springfield model, built in the Massachusetts town of the same name. Its wheels

were manufactured by the Wire Wheel Corporation of America, located in Buffalo, New York, and were

distinctive because of the recessed center portion of the hub nut. A special tool, supplied as one of the twenty-seven

items in the tool box, fit the shape of this recess and permitted removal of the wheel.

■ The engine compartment of a 1947 Delahaye is accessible through an exquisitely

shaped hood, its twin lids opening like wings. In the picture below, left, the long valve cover of its straight six is topped by

a parallel row of brightly polished carburetors, a combination that suggests a powerful elegance.

The engine compartment of a 1916 Simplex, right, surrounds a well-orchestrated display of iron, brass and copper.

At the bottom of the page is a close-up of the heart of a 1915 Rolls-Royce Silver Ghost.

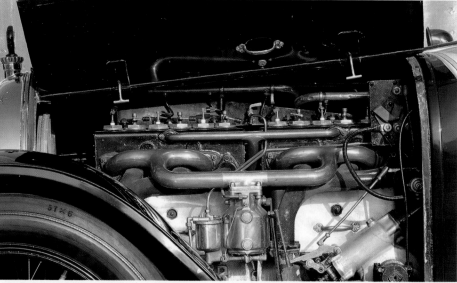

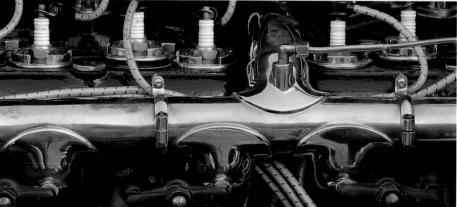

■ Seen here is one of the most outstanding engines of all time, the supercharged Duesenberg SJ. This is not the standard 320-hp version, however, but one fitted with the "rams-horn" intake manifold that breathed through two carburetors—in contrast to the standard SJ supercharger, which used only one. Said to increase engine output from 320 hp to as much as 400, the system was initially developed for the "Duesenberg Special" Land Speed Record car but was later installed on a handful of SJs.

PART THREE

THE AUTOMOBILES

DAIMLER

MODEL 45 CONVERTIBLE SALOON

■ Daimler stands for distinction in more ways than one. Not only can the lineage of this British stalwart be traced back to the birth of the automobile, it can also count a royal connection like no other. ■ In 1888, two years after Gottlieb Daimler's first automobile appeared on the dusty roads of Cannstatt, Germany, Englishman Frederick Simms arranged a meeting with the inventor. Duly impressed, he acquired the British rights to Daimler's engines. In 1893, Simms formed the Daimler Motor Syndicate, only to sell it three years later. The new owners invited Gottlieb Daimler to become a member of the board, a post he held for two years, by which time the first all-British Daimler had been built. ■ The connection with the Crown commenced virtually the moment the Daimler appeared; in 1898, the Prince of Wales was treated to his first demonstration tour over open roads. Two years later, seven months before the death of Queen Victoria, the Prince ordered three Daimlers. Upon ascending the throne to become King Edward VII, his Daimlers ascended with him, becoming the first to inhabit the royal garage. It was an association that would continue unbroken for more than half a century. ■ By the outbreak of World War I, Daimler had compiled a track record of incredible variation. The firm had produced engines with displacements stretching from less than one liter to more than ten, in configurations ranging from

simple side-valve twins to sixes sporting the complex sleeve-valve system adopted in 1909. The types of vehicles produced were no less varied; in addition to the grand royal coaches, there was an array of stately touring machines, as well as, at the opposite end of the spectrum, buses and other commercial vehicles. ■ The post-war years began with a limited selection. One of the two types offered was the Model 45, of which the Collection's Windover-bodied example is a typical illustration—although with a twist. This exquisite automobile was ordered by the Maharajah of Alewar, whose marital arrangement necessitated frequent countryside outings, occasions requiring a certain amount of privacy—this, it is alleged, explains the presence of the finely crafted wooden blinds. ■ The Model 45's six-cylinder sleeve-valve engine has a bore and stroke of 110 mm by 130, a displacement of 7.4 liters (452 cubic inches) and an output of 65 hp at 1400 rpm. Its wheelbase is an impressive 146 inches. Daimler went on to build a pair of progressive overhead-valve V-8s, as well as a massive V-12—mastadons powering some of the most elephantine expressions of the coachbuilder's craft. ■ A unifying element distinguishing all Daimler cars since 1904 has been their fluted radiator shell. Although Daimler was absorbed by Jaguar in 1960, this trademark of tradition still graces the models produced by its new owners.

LA NEF

THREE-WHEELER

■ The three-wheeler has been around since the earliest days of self-propelled vehicles. In fact, the first such vehicle to move successfully under its own power is thought to have been the 1771 steam-engined gun carriage built by Frenchman Nicolas Cugnot, the humble son of a farmer whose crude design featured two wheels at the rear and one up front. ■ The ease with which the steering function could be engineered seems to have been a deciding factor behind several pioneers' choice of the three-wheel layout. This was certainly the case when Carl Benz built his first self-propelled vehicle in 1886—the progenitor of the modern automobile. ■ The same system was also chosen by French pioneers Albert de Dion and Georges Bouton, who in 1895 fitted a gasoline engine of their own design to a three-wheeler. Engines of De Dion-Bouton manufacture were ultimately used in a large number of automobiles worldwide—160 by 1914. Among these were many famous names, such as Sunbeam and Humber in Great Britain and Pierce-Arrow and Peerless in the United States. ■ An obscure and virtually forgotten customer of the De Dion-Bouton powerplant was a Frenchman named La Croix, an eccentric inventor and sometime photographer who, in 1899, established the firm of La Croix de Laville in Agen, France. Its purpose was to facilitate manufacture of a vehicle based on a prototype he had built that year—a curious

three-wheeler. ■ La Croix placed the one-cylinder, 8-hp engine up front in a wooden frame whose two longitudinal members curved inwards as well as upwards, coming to a point above the single front wheel. Steering was controlled through a tiller, which, with a length of 63 inches, must have been something of a record. The wheelbase measured 86 inches. ■ Power was transmitted through a Bozier gearbox to the right-rear wheel via belt drive. The driver, who occupied the left side of the vehicle and steered with his right hand, could affect road speed in two ways—by regulating the throttle or by adjusting the tension of the belt; controls for both of which were located on the left-hand side. The brakes, acting on the rear wheels only, were operated via a foot pedal. Topping off this eccentric piece of machinery was a four-place body with the two rear seats accessible only from the rear. Top speed is not known, but prudence should have kept it low. ■ The La Nef—a fancy French word for ship—probably attracted more smiles than admiration: Imagine the driver attempting to negotiate a sharp turn, a maneuver that would have required either leaning outside the car in a dramatic fashion or sliding across to the other side of the seat. The fact that the peculiar vehicle was still available as late as 1914—by which time some 200 had been built—can only be attributed to the endearing quality of French humor.

MINERVA

TYPE AC DUAL-COWL PHAETON

■ Minerva, "the Goddess of Automobiles," grew out of the humble beginnings of a bicycle manufacturing business founded in Antwerp, Belgium, by Dutchman Sylvain de Jong. Incorporated in 1895, the firm introduced its first series-built automobile in 1904. The Knight sleeve-valve system was adopted in 1909, and on the strength of its product, Minerva went on to become Belgium's largest manufacturer, with an annual production, in 1913, of some 3000 units. ■ During the war, de Jong retreated to his native Holland, where he laid plans for a postwar line of automobiles. This included a monobloc four, introduced in 1919, a six, unveiled in 1920, and a small four, appearing in 1922. ■ Production soon reached prewar levels, and by the mid-Twenties, Minerva had earned a reputation matching those of Rolls-Royce, Hispano-Suiza, Isotta Fraschini and others in the upper-crust category. As with its competitors, Minerva encouraged the leading coachbuilders of the day to execute their craft on the Belgian aristocrat, although a variety of in-house bodies were also built, utilizing a facility in the Antwerp suburb of Mortsel. ■ Responsible for placing Minerva firmly on the map was the famous Type AC, introduced in 1926. Power came from a six-cylinder engine, sporting a bore and stroke of 90 mm by 140, a displacement of 5.8 liters (354 cubic inches) and an output of 82 hp at 2200 rpm. Cradling this fine machine

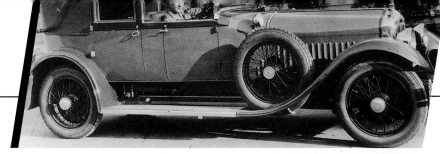

was a frame suspended by semi-elliptic springs front and rear on a 147-inch wheelbase. Brakes were of the highest caliber, servo-assisted, and utilizing huge 17-inch drums. Its transmission was a three-speed affair and top speed was around 90 mph. The example featured in the Collection carries a body by Rollston, the famous Manhattan-based coachbuilding firm. ■ Silent operation became the most famous feature of the Minerva engine, a result of its double sleeve-valve system. But the design also had its drawbacks. Most noticeable—and often the subject of jokes—was the fact that a trail of smoke would emanate from the exhaust pipe, especially during acceleration. Also, while the engine was extremely durable, once in need of repair, the procedure was both complicated and costly. ■ If a potential customer was disuaded by these peculiarities, he could perhaps be persuaded by the design of the radiator and hood—with its unique concave recesses—for it was one of the truly beautiful examples of the contemporary state of steel sculpture. ■ The fortunes of Minerva changed with the death of de Jong in 1928. Subsequent models, powered by straight-eights, perpetuated Minerva's reputation for providing the finest in engineering and coachbuilding. But without de Jong to guide it, Minerva, soon confronted with dwindling sales brought on by the Depression, was marked for a slow death.

UNIC

SERIES C9 LANDAULET TAXI

■ Fame, in the automotive arena, has been won in many ways. Countless inventors, builders and backers have waited in vain for this elusive asset to present itself at their doorstep. Others have had it fall into their lap, while others yet have simply done their thing, inexorably earning their moment in the limelight. ■ A car could become famous simply because it was spectacularly ugly, or, more often, because it was beautiful. The introduction of break-through technical innovations was always a sure road to recognition. The most glorious path of all, however, was one many attempted but few conquered—the race track. But there were other paths, too. ■ The French Unic was not particularly beautiful, ugly, breathtaking or fast, but it was unique—as its name implies—in the sense that its claim to fame was staked in a most undistin-guished field, that of the taxi. Such was its prowess for this line of work that between 1904 and 1912, half of the 7292 Unic taxis built went across the Channel to London—a territory, one would think, a bit hostile to a non-British product. ■ The father of the Unic was Frenchman Georges Ricard, whose first automotive ven-ture ended after an injury in the infamous 1903 Paris-Madrid race. With financial assistance from Baron Henri de Rothschild, Ricard was back in business by the following year. In 1908, the firm—operating under the name Société des Automobiles Unic—could

count forty-nine agents in its homeland and twenty overseas. A contemporary table of total production in France listed Unic second only to Renault. ■ World War I became the arena for another of Unic's claims to fame; during the Marne offensive, when troops were desperately needed at the front, five battalions were ferried there in taxis—an overwhelming number of which were Unics. The Collection's example can lay further claims to fame; this endur-ing workhorse served in London for nearly half a century. It was fi-nally taken out of circulation in 1955, only to appear in the films "My Fair Lady" and "Star." ■ The Unic was powered by a side-valve four, featuring a bore and stroke of 75 mm by 110, a dis-placement of 2.0 liters (118 cubic inches) and an output of 15 hp at 1500 rpm. Its three-speed gearbox was non-synchromesh. The rear-wheel brakes were pedal actuated, while a hand lever oper-ated a transmission brake. The wheelbase measured 106 inches. The weight, of the chassis only, was 1455 pounds. Equipped with a turning radius that endeared it to an entire generation of cab driv-ers, the Unic was rugged and nearly indestructible. ■ Unic manu-factured other cars besides taxis, but these never attained fame. Production instead was gradually steered towards commercial ve-hicles. After becoming a cog in the Fiat empire in 1975, the Unic name struggled on until 1983.

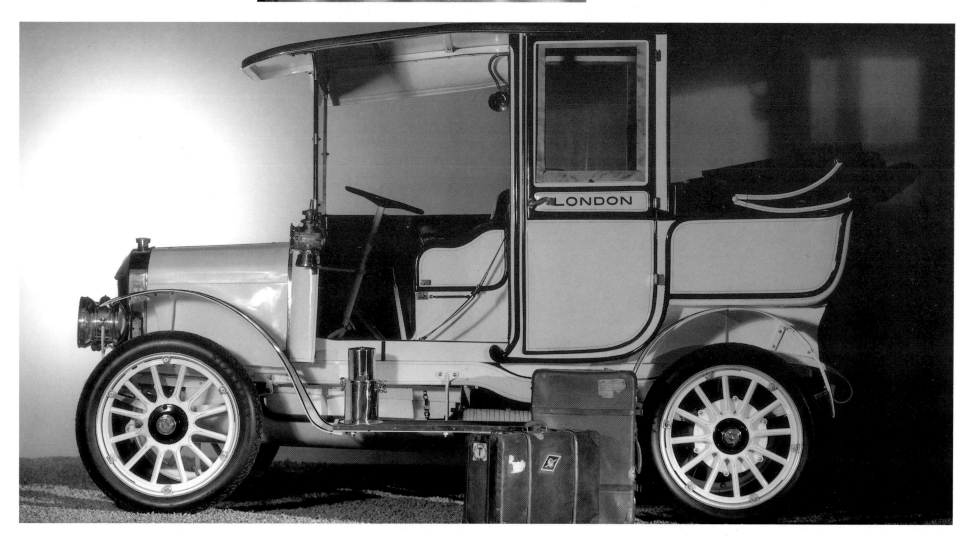

CORD

MODEL L-29 CABRIOLET

■ *To imagine the era of the great classics without Auburn, Cord and Duesenberg is to imagine the films of the Thirties without Garbo, Gable and Harlow; in either case, much of the glamour would be gone.* ■ *The power behind these magnificent cars was generated almost entirely by one man: Errett Lobban Cord. In 1924, Cord, only thirty years old, had taken over management of stagnating Auburn. Sales soared immediately, energized primarily by cosmetic changes.* ■ *By 1929, Cord had gained control of the company. Flush with success, he went after Duesenberg. The firm had fallen on hard times and lacked the capital to develop a new model. Soon Cord's injection of cash and his inspiring vision brought forth the legendary Model J.* ■ *But there was more to come. Cord needed a product to fill the gap between the low-end Auburn and the high-end Duesenberg. It would have front-wheel drive. And it would carry the Cord name. That the Indianapolis successes of Harry Miller's front-wheel-drive racers had influenced Cord became obvious when he bought the patent rights in 1927. Cord soon assembled an engineering team and sent it to work at Miller's Los Angeles shop.* ■ *By the end of 1928, the action had moved to Indianapolis; the chassis was ready to receive a body, and Auburn designer John Oswald proved the man for the task. The result was the most striking automobile of its day. Measuring just 50*

inches from the road to the top of its hood, the machine stood ten inches lower than the competition. ■ Contributing further to its rakish look was the long sweep of the hood, a feature necessitated by the length of the engine, which had been turned back to front, locating the transmission ahead of the block. The hood could have been even longer; the engine penetrated six inches into the driver's compartment. ■ The L-29's side-valve, straight-eight power source, built by Lycoming—a company also owned by Cord—had a bore and stroke of 3.3 inches by 4.5, a displacement of 299 cubic inches (4.9 liters) and an output of 115 hp at 3300 rpm. The three-speed, non-synchromesh transmission was operated via a dashboard-mounted handle. Top speed of the 137.5-inch wheelbase, 4620-pound package was less than 80 mph—making its allure not so much a matter of being fast, but looking fast. ■ Sales met with resistance, but this was less the result of problems related to front-wheel drive than it was directly connected with the Crash—coming only three months after the L-29's introduction. The original price of $3295—for the Cabriolet—was soon lowered to $2495. . . in vain. By the middle of 1932, after 4429 had been built, the conveyor of the Cord name was put to rest—but not permanently. A few years hence the appellation would be resurrected for yet another masterpiece—the Cord 810.

MERCEDES

MODEL 8/18 TOWN CAR

■ During the first decade of the twentieth century, Daimler and Benz—who would join forces as Daimler-Benz in 1926—still functioned separately, both pursuing the perfection of their individual products. Daimler was the more prominent of the two, however, as the Cannstatt firm possessed the brilliant engineering talent of Wilhelm Maybach and Paul Daimler. Yet it is unlikely that the road to success would have run so straight had it not been for Emil Jellinek, a colorful entrepreneur whose playground was Nice on the French Riviera. ■ Having placed an order for four cars with Daimler in 1896, Jellinek soon bought six more, which put him in a position to make constructive suggestions about the product, such as moving the engine from the middle to the front, enlarging it from two to four ylinders in the process—the automobile would never be the same. ■ In 1890, with the cars duly revised, Jellinek entered one of them in the Nice-La Turbie hillclimb. The result was not glory but disaster, with a crash killing the driver. Undaunted, Jellinek blamed the car and suggested further improvements, backing his request with a third order—this time for thirty-six. He also demanded that the new model be named Mercedes, after one of his daughters. ■ The Mercedes was a sensation; the 1901 Nice Week, which incorporated a long distance race, a sprint and a hillclimb, saw the newcomer win all three events. Followed

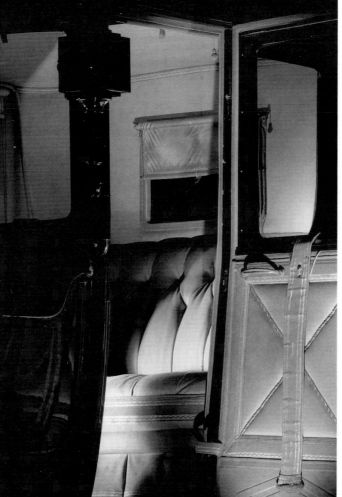

by many more victories, this coup helped to form a foundation for commercial success. ■ Among those watching the events from this side of the Atlantic was multi-millionaire William Kissam Vanderbilt. Having purchased one of the earliest Mercedes cars in 1901, he three years later took delivery of another—a powerful Type 90 racer—and proceeded to Ormond Beach, Florida, where he covered the flying mile at a speed of 92 mph, traveling faster than any man before him. Again, racing generated sales and Mercedes became the best-selling imported car in America. ■ Another Mercedes enthusiast and multi-millionaire was John Jacob Astor, whose fortune rested on Manhattan real estate. One of the cars in his Mercedes stable has survived and is featured here, an exquisite town car bodied by Belvallette of Paris. Built in 1909—the year in which the three-pointed star first appeared on the radiator—it remains in original condition, its luxurious cloth interior giving off the unmistakable scent of history. In contrast to its imposing dimensions, its four-cylinder engine produced a moderate 18 hp at 1200 rpm. ■ John Jacob Astor went down with the Titanic on that fateful night in 1912. His Mercedes remained in the family, stored for more than four decades in a Bronx warehouse. Later, the heirs moved the car to the family estate in Florida, from where it was brought to the Collection.

C A D I L L A C

MODEL 452A DUAL-COWL PHAETON

■ As the Roaring Twenties churned inexorably towards a tumultuous climax, an ever-escalating stock market made millionaires out of common people. Flappers and movie stars, bootleggers and gangsters all became symbols of an era that knew no limits. ■ The luxury automobile flourished in this climate. Yet the golden age of coachbuilding demanded larger, more powerful engines to carry heavier, more elaborate bodies. With conventional straight-eights stretched to their rough-running limits, smoothness became the catchword. The move towards the ultimate machine, the sixteen, had begun. ■ It fell to Larry Fisher, new head of Cadillac in 1925, and his man in charge of engine development, Owen Nacker, to create the first American V-16. In Europe, Ettore Bugatti had conceived a sixteen-cylinder aircraft engine in 1917. The U.S. Government was interested, and the man sent to investigate, Howard Marmon—who would introduce his own sixteen in 1931—gave the thumbs up. Duesenberg was awarded the contract, but by the time the engine stood ready to enter production, the war was over and only eleven units resulted. ■ Marmon and Nacker were good friends; when Fisher called, Nacker had already given much thought to a V-16. Its final design placed the cylinders in a 45-degree vee. Bore and stroke measured 3.0 inches by 4.0, producing a displacement of 7.4 liters, or 452 cubic inches—the source, as

was the Cadillac style, of its official designation. Two overhead valves per cylinder were operated through pushrods and rockers, commanded by a camshaft located in the center of the vee. Output was 165 hp at 3400 rpm. With a weight of around 6000 pounds, the 148-inch-wheelbase, three-speed-transmission package managed about 90 mph. ■ Cadillac's goal for the Sixteen, however, was not so much performance as it was prestige—a commodity partly attributable to Harley Earl's styling. His inspiration came from Europe and the Hispano-Suiza. But it was not merely a matter of transference—Earl's talent was too great. From the huge head-lamps, to the smooth fenderline, to the upturned rear—it was all Earl, all elegance. ■ By the time the Sixteen faced the public in January 1930, Wall Street's darkest hour still cast its doomsday shadows. But work continued in the Fleetwood facilities and by June 1930, 2000 cars had been built. The last half of the year saw another 887. The following year added a final 364. The Collection's example carried a price tag of $6500, and represents one of only 85 Fleetwood-bodied phaetons. ■ Unlike many of its peers, Cadillac survived the Crash. Its V-16 went on to power a succession of restyled models, staying in production until 1937, when a new, less complex version carried the torch for three more years. That, as they say, was the end of an era.

LOCOMOBILE

MODEL 48 TOURING

■ Locomobile—one of the most esteemed American luxury cars of its day—began and ended with confusion. In 1899, John Brisben Walker, owner of Cosmopolitan magazine, and Amzi Lorenzo Barber, of Barber Asphalt Company, formed the Automobile Company of America, only to discover that the name had already been taken. Their second choice—the Locomobile Company of America—suggested that the fledgling firm was off to an uncertain start. ■ The company had been formed to purchase the original Stanley steamer, which it did. But the partners soon quarreled, splitting up before the end of the year. Walker went on to build the Mobile, while Barber continued the Locomobile venture, consolidating it in Bridgeport, Connecticut, in 1902. Some 5000 steamers had been manufactured when, in 1903, the model was replaced by a gasoline-powered car designed by Andrew Lawrence Riker. ■ By this time, the Stanley brothers were back with an improved version of their original design. Locomobile, with Riker on board, was also ready to move. ■ Riker's first Locomobile was inspired by Mercedes, and it seemed only natural for the company to emulate its guiding star by embarking on a racing effort. In 1906, a massive four-cylinder, 17-liter, 120-hp monster made its debut at the Vanderbilt Cup, a race first run on New York's Long Island in 1904. European cars had dominated the event, and Riker's crea-

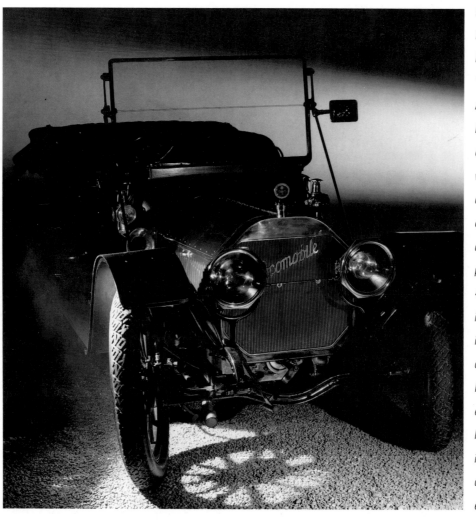

tion did not change that situation until 1908, when George Robertson brought a Locomobile—with a huge 16 painted on the hood and radiator—first across the finish line. This machine—"Old No. 16"—survived to become a beloved symbol of early American racing. ■ Locomobile capitalized on its reputation by building a series of fine cars, but it was not until 1911 that the company hit its stride, introducing the famous Model 48—of which the Collection's specimen is an outstanding first-year example. ■ Power came from a pair-cast, T-head six, featuring a crankshaft with seven main bearings. Bore and stroke were square at 4.5 inches, displacement 429 cubic inches (7.0 liters) and output 48 hp at 2200 rpm. Built like a battleship, the imposing Model 48 rolled on a 135-inch wheelbase and could reach 60 mph using its four-speed gearbox. The price—for the seven-passenger touring body—was an even $4800. ■ The Model 48 stayed in production until the bitter end in 1929. The years following World War I had dealt the Locomobile a series of blows that gradually weakened its prestige. The final injustice was administered when William Crapo Durant bought the company in 1922, and proceeded to introduce a cheap Junior Eight—a move that diluted its reputation and dealt a deadly punch to an automobile that had once been the embodiment of its slogan: "Easily The Best-Built Car in America."

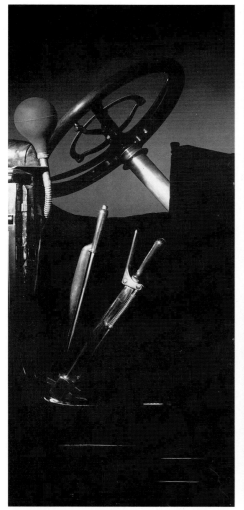

HORCH

TYP 670 SPORT CABRIOLET

■ August Horch, born in 1868, looms large in the annals of German auto manufacture. His influence embraces not only the firm that made his name famous, established in 1899, but also another important marque, Audi, founded a decade later. ■ The record of Horch's early career illustrates the tightly woven world of the pioneers. His first experience came during a three-year stint as an engineer in the employ of Carl Benz. After Horch had been forced out of the firm bearing his name in 1900, Paul Daimler—the son of fellow pioneer Gottlieb Daimler—became its chief engineer. Another thread leads to Fritz Fiedler, who headed Horch's ambitious V-12 project in the early Thirties before going on to further fame in the halls of BMW, where he engineered such immortal sporting machines as the 328 and the 507. ■ In the mid-Twenties, Horch had been the first in Germany to feature straight-eight power. This had been a period of confidence, but a few years later, on the threshold of a new decade, Horch's management suffered from disillusionment after its product was eclipsed by Mercedes-Benz's fabulous flagship, the 770K, and Maybach's magnificent engineering triumph, the Zeppelin. The decision was made to try to outmaneuver the rivals with a V-12-powered mastadon, the Type 600, a long-wheelbase, limousine-style automobile first exhibited at the Paris Salon in the fall of 1931. ■ But while the product was well

thought out, the timing was not, and only twenty 600s were built. The V-12 engine also found its way into the Type 670, which rested on a shorter, 125-inch wheelbase. Produced between 1931 and 1934, the 670—of which just 58 were built—was available in two open versions. ■ Fiedler's 60-degree, single-overhead-cam V-12 sported a bore and stroke of 80 mm by 100, a displacement of an even 6.0 liters (368 cubic inches) and an output of 120 hp at 3200 rpm, which gave the 5390-pound five-seater a top speed of 85 mph. The four-speed transmission featured a world first: synchromesh in all four gears. ■ The 670 shown here carries the characteristic windshield with angled corner windows, drawn by Horch's own Hermann Ahrens and built by the Glachau-based firm of Dietzsch. One of only three known survivors, the rare machine was added to the Collection in 1987 after having been purchased at that year's Sotheby Auction in Geneva. ■ In 1933, August Horch made a triumphant return to the organization he had left twenty-four years earlier. During the next few years, he led the Zwickau-based firm into a period of final greatness. The outbreak of war, however, put a halt to automobile production, and the emphasis shifted to the manufacture of troop carriers. No cars were built after the war, and August Horch retired to a small town in Bavaria, where he died in 1951.

DETROIT ELECTRIC

MODEL 46 ROADSTER

■ In the early days of motoring, two alternative propulsion methods competed with the internal combustion engine for the attention of a booming market—steam and electricity. The manufacturers of electric vehicles touted the clean, quiet and safe operation of their product, and the points they made were certainly strong ones.

■ In Great Britain, the London Electric Cab Company was already operating a fleet of 75 electric taxis by 1897. At the turn of the century, electric cabs also became popular in New York, Boston and other American cities. By 1907, Columbia—the Hartford-built electric—had supplied some 9000 taxis to various East Coast communities. ■ The electric era reached its zenith in the period immediately preceding World War I. At that time, while the Baker Electric—one of the most successful brands—had already begun its slide towards extinction, the most prominent of the breed, the Detroit Electric, was still going strong, with some 3000 units emerging from the Detroit factory in 1916. ■ The firm had its roots in the Anderson Carriage Company, established in 1884. Its founder, William Anderson, had been slow to move his business out of the horse-drawn era, but when he did so in 1907, his choice came down on the side of electricity. George Bacon was the designer of the first Detroit, whose popularity led to rapid domination of the market: From 126 units in the first year, output rose to

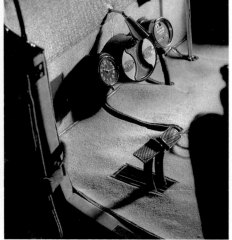

1500 in 1910. The following year saw the introduction of "Direct Shaft Drive," with chain drive still remaining optional. ■ The Detroit had its motor located in the middle, while the batteries—weighing all of 1000 pounds—were placed both up front and at the rear. The company was careful to tell its customers that the car was not a touring vehicle. Its range was typically advertised as 80 miles between charges, although, in a pickle, special optional adaptor cables made it possible to zap needed juice from the overhead wires of trolley cars. Its power rating was about 5 hp, top speed circa 12 mph. The Collection's Roadster, priced at $2500, was one of six models offered in 1914, all riding on a 100-inch wheelbase. With its ease of operation—there was no starting handle—the Detroit became especially attractive to lady drivers.

■ While the demand for electrics dropped rapidly after World War I, Detroit stayed alive by shifting its emphasis to commercial vehicles. As late as 1926, however, one could still buy a Detroit brougham that looked essentially the same as it had a decade earlier. Yet, starting in the Thirties, and continuing up to the end in 1939, Detroit offered a most curious creature—a conventional body, supplied by Willys-Overland, sporting a hood and grille from Dodge. It was the last desperate gasp of a dying breed, one that had seen the rise and fall of the original urban vehicle.

PIERCE-ARROW

■ In the early Thirties, it was widely believed that the time for streamlined automobiles had come. It was thought that soon, perhaps within a decade, all cars would look like teardrops. ■ The earliest impulses came from Europe, where Swiss scientist Paul Jaray—constructing bizarre cars that excelled in theoretical accuracy but lacked artistic flair—had become something of a guru. In America, interest was spurred by the experiments of aircraft pioneer Glenn Curtiss, who in 1928 performed wind-tunnel tests with conventional cars. ■ The auto industry watched with interest, but moved cautiously. Then, in 1932, former GM stylist Phil Wright approached Pierce-Arrow with a proposal for a sweepingly futuristic design. ■ At the time it was common knowledge that Pierce-Arrow was on the ropes. Four years earlier, it had been forced to accept a merger with Studebaker, but the downward drift had continued and by 1932 production had sunk to 2692 units. Management was desperate. In October, they accepted Wright's proposal.

■ Only five units were to be built—in secrecy, and in a hurry. The needed chassis were immediately shipped from Buffalo to South Bend, where the Studebaker engineering department gathered a team of three dozen craftsmen. Chief body engineer James Hughes, given a deadline only three months away, was placed in charge. Working around the clock, the seemingly impossible task

was accomplished on time. ■ When Wright, who had been cut out of the process, saw the finished product, he realized his original design had been tampered with. Hughes had exchanged the original rear end for one from a Studebaker show car that included a small, vee-shaped window. Further reason for the altered design lay with the contraction required by a change to a 139-inch wheelbase from the 147-inch length originally specified. Otherwise, Wright's shape was intact, with faired-in headlights, flowing pontoon-like front fenders carrying concealed spare wheels and teardrop-shaped rear fenders with full-length skirts. ■ Power came from Pierce-Arrow's L-head V-12, featuring a bore and stroke of 3.5 inches by 4.0, a displacement of 462 cubic inches (7.6 liters) and an output of 175 hp at 3400 rpm. The unit propelled the 5729-pound car to a top speed of 115 mph. The transmission was a three-speed gearbox equipped with a free-wheeling device. ■ The Silver Arrow owned by the Collection was shipped to Buffalo on February 11, 1933. It still stands as it did back then, untouched, except for its paint. The first Silver Arrow was sent to the New York Auto Show, where it caused a sensation. Although a show stopper, it failed to save the company. Probably nothing, short of a miracle, could have done that. But the Silver Arrow was as close to a miracle as anyone could have come.

RENAULT

TYPE JD 40CV COUPE CONVERTIBLE

■ When Jean-Pierre Jabouille led Renault's Formula One team to victory in the 1979 French Grand Prix, the feat provided a compelling counterpoint to the past achievements of a marque that, seven decades earlier, campaigned a thirteen-liter monster—with Francois Szisz at the wheel—to the finish line of the first-ever Grand Prix, run at the Sarthe circuit near Le Mans in 1906. ■ It all began with Louis Renault, born in Paris in 1877, the son of a draper. Dropping out of school, he turned his back on the family business and built his first automobile in 1898. Production was not even contemplated until the prodding of friends forced a limited run that lead to the 1899 formation of Renault Frères. ■ A dozen years later Renault had grown to become France's largest automaker, turning out more than 10,000 cars annually with a work force of almost 4000. World War I prompted further expansion, brought on by a huge output of trucks, tanks and aero engines. By the end of the war, in 1918, the work force had grown to 22,500, and the Billancourt facilities near Paris covered 87 acres. ■ The postwar range of cars consisted of three fours and a six. Foremost among them was one of the greatest Renaults ever, the 40CV, a machine whose majestic proportions rivaled the most magnificent of the era, and one preferred by many celebrities: the Collection's example belonged to France's battlefield hero, General Foch. The

■ A RADICAL RENAULT ROADSTER READY FOR A HOLLYWOOD SCREEN TEST

40CV was introduced in 1921 and reflected its creator's autocratic rule by retaining the cowl-positioned radiator and the scuttle-style hood. ■ Power came from a sidevalve six of massive proportions—bore and stroke were 110 mm by 160, creating a displacement of 9.1 liters (564 cubic inches) and an output 140 hp at 2700 rpm. Thanks to the ample torque, the 40CV's top speed of 80 mph was reached with minimal use of its four-speed transmission. The brakes, operating on all four wheels, were servo-driven off the gearbox. The Kellner-bodied beauty pictured here rolls on a 158-inch wheelbase and weighs 6100 pounds. ■ The 40CV lasted until 1928, by which time it was thoroughly outdated. A new range of straight eights—with their radiators located in a more conventional position—carried Renault into the Thirties.

■ The outbreak of World War II triggered the tragic demise of Louis Renault. Convinced the conflict would soon be over, he refused a French government request to enter military production. After the German occupation, however, the transition was made by force, and Renault spent the war years building trucks for the Wehrmacht. Liberation and its need for revenge saw him thrown in jail as a collaborator. Denied medical attention, he died in 1944. Shortly thereafter his empire was nationalized and a former resistance hero installed as its head.

DUESENBERG

MODEL SJ DUAL-COWL PHAETON

■ *In spite of the fame of the Duesenberg race car—the first and only American machine to have won the French Grand Prix—its companion road car, as marketed during most of the Twenties, failed to generate the excitement produced by its competition counterpart.* ■ *This was partly a result of its coachwork, which took its cue from men whose minds were crowded by issues of engineering and failed to match the effervescence of the machinery. It was with the 1926 arrival of E. L. Cord, and his inspiring dream of creating an automobile on a grand scale, that the Duesenberg reached its zenith.* ■ *The emergence of Duesenberg as "The World's Finest Motor Car" could not have happened without the engineering genius of Fred Duesenberg. It is equally clear that the feat would never have been accomplished without the financial backing and inspired guidance of Cord. Likewise, without Gordon Buehrig—the designer who, at age twenty-five, became responsible for the Duesenberg look—the circles combining form and function would never have been so perfectly joined.* ■ *The man whose prolific pen would give shape to more than half of all Duesenbergs produced went from high school in Peoria, Illinois, through courses in drafting, art and metal shop at Bradley College, to an apprenticeship at the Gotfredson Body Company in Wayne, Michigan. Further turns on the road to Duesenberg were negoti-*

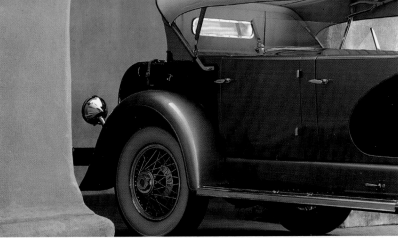

ated at Packard, General Motors and Stutz. ■ Harold Ames, Duesenberg's sales manager, was responsible for hiring Buehrig. Ames was also the man who, together with Cord and Auburn designer Al Leamy, established the shape that defined the Duesenberg look, such as the radiator shell, the hood and the fenders. Only the mascot was Buehrig's creation. ■ The lines of the La Grande dual-cowl phaeton represented here became something of a Duesenberg trademark with its characteristic "sweep panel" that flowed from the hood down across the front doors. Buehrig's inspiration for the La Grande came from a design created by Le Baron, but it was Buehrig's genius that elevated the shape to its level of artistic perfection. ■ The builder, the Union City Body Company of Union City, Indiana, was not a prestige carriage house. In a classic example of salesmanship, Ames invented the La Grande name, adding a touch of acquired class. Delivered to Duesenberg's Indianapolis facility in the white, the bodies were finished by in-house craftsmen. The chassis demanded a stately $8500, with the body adding $4000 to $6500. ■ The Duesenberg shown here first carried a sedate sedan body. Later, when more power and flashier coachwork was desired, the engine received a supercharger and the chassis a La Grande-style body, one that in its superb execution emulates all the grace and beauty of the original.

SANDFORD

TYPE S CYCLECAR

■ In its infancy, the automobile constituted an exclusive form of transportation, available only to the man of considerable means. Its development at first centered around finding the upper limits of the machine and not on simplification for mass production—a fact only perpetuating the elusiveness of motorized mobility for the man of lesser means. ■ After the turn of the century, however, there appeared a new breed, a type of automobile called a "cyclecar." Usually based on motorcycle components, the cyclecar was small and simply constructed and therefore cheap to build. The concept inspired a slew of sporty little machines both in England and on the Continent, and the craze even swept across to the U.S. ■ In 1913, the tiny Morgan scored a sensational win in the French Cyclecar Grand Prix at Amiens, creating an immediate interest in the British manufacturer and its three-wheel design. Capitalizing on this attention was one Malcolm Stuart Sandford—an Englishman born in Birmingham—who built a successful business around his Paris-based Morgan agency. ■ In 1922, Sandford initiated manufacture of his own car. Subsequent racing successes created a small but ready market, and by 1925 the firm—well established in the Paris suburb of Levallois-Perret—employed twelve workers. Production peaked during 1926 and 1927, with an annual output of around 50 units. ■ Sandford's high point came at

a time when the cyclecar—especially popular in France where automobiles displacing less than 1100 cc enjoyed a favored tax status—had virtually disappeared, replaced by the early progeny of mass production. The Collection's example typifies the marque at its peak of popularity. Power came from the French-built Ruby, a fierce little water-cooled four that, in its most sporting form, reportedly produced as much as 50 hp from its 1.1-liter (68-cubic-inch) displacement. A three-speed gearbox, operated via a stubby, floor-mounted lever, was in unit with the engine, whose power was transported to the driving wheel via chain drive. Brakes, at first fitted only on the rear wheel, were added up front starting in 1924.

■ The sleek, door-less aluminum body rested on a 97-inch wheelbase, and featured an intimate cockpit whose Spartan environment was dominated by a 20-inch steering wheel. The dash sported a handsome set of Jaeger gauges, including speedometer, tachometer and clock. Its top speed, in racing trim, is thought to have been as much as 100 mph—a frightening pace for such a diminutive vehicle. ■ After 1936, by which time some 300 Sandfords had been built, production trickled to a halt, with a final blow administered by the outbreak of World War II. The Sandford was one of the last survivors of the cyclecar phenomenon—a breed that first brought the thrill of motoring to the common man.

HISPANO-SUIZA

TYPE J12 TRANSFORMABLE

■ The name Hispano-Suiza refers to Spain, where the marque originated, and to Switzerland, the birthplace of Marc Birkigt, whose engineering brilliance guided Hispano from the beginning to the end. ■ Birkigt's offspring earned a reputation as a first among equals, an epithet stemming not only from their remarkable engineering but also from the bodies created for them by the world's finest coachbuilders—an amalgam of the best of both disciplines. ■ Hispano referred to its product as "The Queen of Automobiles." It might have been more appropriate, however, to have adopted the appellation of "King"—Spain's Alfonso XIII acquired a Hispano in 1905 and later allowed a model to carry his name. ■ The roots of the Alfonso were found in a racer that won France's "Coup de l'Auto" in 1910. The success created a demand among French buyers and a subsidiary was set up in Paris. The factory at first occupied an old tram depot alongside the Seine in Levallois-Perret, but was later moved to a facility in Bois-Colombes, from which all of the classic Hispanos originated. ■ During World War I, Hispano's manufacturing emphasis switched to aircraft engines, an involvement inspiring the most famous of the Hispano automobiles, the H6, with its fabulous overhead-cam, six-cylinder power plant. ■ The climax—some say the anti-climax—was reached in 1931 with the V-12 powered J12. Its complex pushrod-

activated valvetrain exchanged the H6's mechanical sophistication for a less exotic but quieter design. Bore and stroke were an even 100 mm by 100, displacement 9.4 liters (575 cubic inches) and output 220 hp at 3000 rpm. ■ The J12 continued the use of Birkigt's legendary servo-assisted brakes, but the three-speed gearbox, with its too-high first gear and the less-than-adequate multiplate clutch, were no match for the 5000-pound giant. Once the initial inertia was overcome, however, the J12 ate up the road— 0 to 60 mph took just 12 seconds. Top speed was around 100 mph. ■ No less than four wheelbases were available, the longest measuring 158 inches. Only 120 J12s had been built when Birkigt put aside automobiles in 1938 to concentrate, once again, on aircraft engines. The Hispano-Suiza badge was never again to grace an automobile. With a postwar world completely changed, Birkigt retired to Switzerland, where he died in 1953. ■ The Collection's J12 features a one-off body by Saoutchik, the prestigious Parisian coachbuilder. Commissioned by a British gentleman named Batcock, its sumptuous passenger compartment boasts a finely crafted cabinet, complete with decanters and glasses as well as a comb and mirror on the ladies side, and cigar box and cutter on the gentleman's side—trappings befitting an automobile that so perfectly reflected the aspirations of the upper crust.

ROLLS-ROYCE

PHANTOM I TRANSFORMABLE

■ A shop on Taylor Street in Springfield, Massachusetts, was the 1895 birthplace of the earliest series-built American automobile, the Duryea. This machine proved of such interest to the British that production was organized in England in 1902. ■ Two decades later, in a reverse parallel, Rolls-Royce decided to set up shop in America, settling in, of all places, Springfield. The selection was made because the city—a site of both rifle and motorcycle factories—boasted a highly skilled labor force. It was, in fact, a former Indian Motorcycle plant that in 1920 became the home of Rolls-Royce of America, Inc. ■ Due to a wave of postwar demand, British Rolls faced a two-year backlog of orders, a problem an American factory would help alleviate. British law prohibited transfer of assets, however, so the American firm was financed by domestic interests. Managers and foremen, on the other hand, were brought over from the Rolls works in Derby. This was done to prevent two sets of standards—a Rolls had to be a Rolls no matter where it was built. ■ That this goal had been met became evident when the first American chassis appeared in 1921; despite the fact that the entire car had been assembled on this side of the Atlantic, the American copy was identical to the original. ■ But when Rolls-Royce of America bought the Brewster coachbuilding firm in 1925—and began to supply complete cars—the character of the

Springfield issue changed considerably, not in quality, but in style. Brewster produced a catalog that listed no less than twenty-eight bodies, which all, appropriately, were named after English towns—such as Oxford, Pickwick and Wimbledon. ■ Mechanically, the Springfield Rolls shared its specifications with the Derby version, the Phantom I engine being an inline six, with a bore and stroke of 108 mm by 140, a displacement of 7.7 liters (470 cubic inches) and an output of 80 hp at 2250 rpm. There were two wheelbase choices available—143.5 inches and 146.5. With 1924 prices for bodied cars ranging from $12,930 to $15,880, the Rolls was America's most expensive car. ■ When the Phantom II arrived in 1929, Springfield could not afford to retool. Imported chassis, mixed with outdated domestic ones, kept the company going until 1934, by which time 2944 cars had been built. ■ The Collection's example features a body by Hibbard & Darrin, the famous Paris-based firm headed by two American expatriates. This created the awkward combination of an American-built chassis being shipped to France—with England just across the channel— then, after application of the coachwork, being shipped back to America. But these were times when the selection of a new automobile was never taken lightly; as with choosing a future bride, the decision was intended to be of lasting duration.

MERCEDES-BENZ

TYP 500K SPEZIAL-ROADSTER

■ The past glory of Mercedes-Benz should weigh heavily on pres-ent-day management as it looks back on the fabulous machines the firm created in the Twenties and Thirties. Perhaps it is no coinci-dence that the company's once common practice of including clas-sics in its advertising seems to have been abandoned. The exclusiv-ity of the handcrafted automobiles, matched by the beauty of their lines, no longer provide flattering comparisons with products from the age of robot technology. ■ It was the 1926 amalgamation of Daimler and Benz that spawned a special breed of Mercedes-Benz sports car. Those were the days of the Ferdinand Porsche-designed SSKs and SSKLs, muscular monsters powered by huge super-charged sixes that swept clean the racing circuits, rip-roaring and tail-spinning their way to immortality. ■ After a period of financial difficulties during the Depression, the early Thirties saw Mercedes-Benz return with vigor. The German economy bustled from the energy of a new political system, one of whose grand projects was the construction of the Autobahn highway network. This challenged Mercedes-Benz to design an automobile capable of sustained high-speed driving. The new breed should not be seen as a sports car in the past sense, but as a machine combining power and elegance as never before. ■ Porsche had left Daimler-Benz in 1928; his place had been taken by Hans Nibel, a veteran from the days of

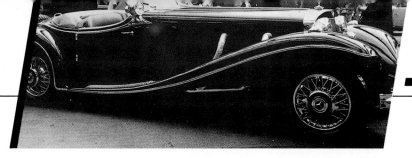

the 1908 Grand Prix Benz. The first of Nibel's designs, introduced in 1933 as the 380, was powered by a 3.8-liter, overhead-valve, straight eight. Found low on power, its displacement was increased to 5.0 liters (306 cubic inches) in 1934, and the model designation changed to 500K—the K denoting the addition of a "Kompressor," or supercharger. ■ The Collection's 500K represents a design first seen at the 1935 Berlin Auto Show. The Spezial-Roadster was the sportiest among a choice of nine bodystyles—drawn by Hermann Ahrens and built by the Stuttgart firm's own Sindelfingen coachworks. Records indicate that only twenty-nine Spezial-Roadsters were produced, a figure that includes an unspecified number of Normal-Roadsters—identified by their flat windscreens. ■ The Spezial-Roadster rests on a 119-inch wheelbase, weighs 4775 pounds, has a four-speed gearbox, servo-assisted hydraulic brakes and fully independent suspension. Bore and stroke are 86 mm by 108, output 100 hp at 3400 rpm—160 hp with the supercharger engaged. ■ A sixteen-second burst jettisons the machine to 60 mph. Another rush brings on the top speed of nearly 100 mph, a figure the driver—if he is able to break the spell of the screaming supercharger—can confirm with a glance at the speedometer, which, as befits this contradiction of elegance and power, is set in a glamorous mother-of-pearl dash.

PACKARD

MODEL 745 CONVERTIBLE COUPE

■ Nineteen twenty-nine began in an atmosphere of buoyancy. The boardrooms of Detroit, a dependable barometer of the nation's mood, were bristling with optimism. Factories were bursting, business was booming. ■ Executives at Dodge, DeSoto and Plymouth patted each other's backs with confident ebullience—their production volume had more than doubled. At Hudson/Essex, the folks were too busy to do anything but attend to business; having produced 280,000 units in 1928, the machinery now churned out cars at a rate equivalent to a year-end total of over 300,000. ■ On East Grand Boulevard, too, the mood was optimistic—Packard had seen its annual registrations swell from around 30,000 in 1927 to nearly 43,000 in 1928. The firm had its feet planted on solid financial ground. ■ The Packard featured on these pages—a model 745, sporting a Derham body of which only three are thought to have been built—represents a paragon of the marque. The Packard look had become a beacon, a status symbol; it seemed impossible to improve. Yet the 1930 model looked better than ever—more rakish, subtly shifted towards a more modern style. Indeed, there had been alterations; the radiator had been slanted one and a half degrees, and it had also been lowered, by an inch and a half. Less subtle was the lengthening of the hood by as much as five inches. ■ Under that sleek new

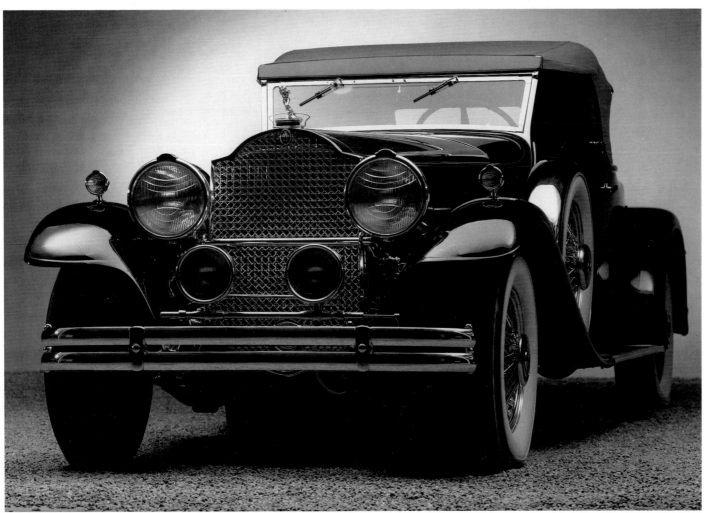

stretch of steel hid Packard's supreme straight-eight, a marvel of smoothness, featuring a bore and stroke of 3.5 inches by 5.0, a displacement of 385 cubic inches (6.3 liters) and an output of 106 hp at 3200 rpm. A four-speed transmission was new for the 1930 model year. The 745 rested on the flagship-size 145.5-inch wheelbase. Cost was in proportion to elegance—no less than eleven bodystyles priced from $4585 to $5350 in addition to the option of coachbuilt exclusivity. ■ The 745 was introduced in August 1929—in October came the Wall Street ticker-tape tragedy. But the show had to go on. In December, the Annual Custom Salon, held at Manhattan's haughty Commodore Hotel, opened as usual. Although the week-long show had the atmosphere of a gala event, behind the scenes coachbuilders faced problems financing their extravagant creations.•■ The year as a whole, however, did produce a new production record for America's automakers—the five million mark was broken for the first time. For Packard, too, 1929 was a record year, and, despite the Crash, the year ended in continued optimism—although tempered by an undercurrent of anxiety. ■ When the totals for 1930 were tallied, the worst fears were verified; Packard production dropped below the 30,000 mark. And things would get worse before they would get better—at the depth of the Depression, in 1934, Packard built just 6000 cars.

MAYBACH

TYP W6 DSG CABRIOLET

■ The least-known among the great European classics, May-bach—manufactured in Friedrichshafen, Germany—carries a particular aura of exclusivity, a distinction that resulted from the limited numbers produced, the uncompromising devotion to quality that characterized their maker and from the substantial price that typically accompanies low-volume production. ■ In a ranking of exclusivity among prewar German luxury automobiles, one would find Mercedes-Benz next to the top, with Horch a notch below. The unchallenged champion would be Maybach—the automobile for the mature gentleman of means who thought the Mercedes-Benz a bit too flamboyant and the Horch a touch too pedestrian. ■ Another aspect of the Maybach aura stems from the complexity of its engineering—a perfect example of the term "over-engineered." The most vivid illustration of excess could be found in its transmission. After having favored a gearbox with just two forward gears since entering automobile manufacture in 1921, Maybach went overboard with its 1929 model, endowing it with a three-speed unit, which, when augmented with an overdrive that could be activated in any gear—including reverse—allowed six forward choices and two reverse. ■ The system was labelled "Schnell-gang," which translates to "Quick-Shift." The extreme development of this complex device came with the "Doppelschnellgang"

or "Double-Quick-Shift," which, in its ultimate form, offered a choice of eight forward speeds and, theoretically, eight reverse.

■ Perhaps the most epic aspect of the Maybach story stems from its Zeppelin connection. The founder of the Maybach works, Wilhelm Maybach, at first concentrated on the manufacture of engines. This led to a venture with Graf Ferdinand von Zeppelin and his dirigibles, for which Maybach's firm supplied motive power. In 1929, at the height of the Zeppelin era, the globe-encircling airship was propelled by no less than five 550-hp Maybach V-12s. These units inspired the firm's automotive V-12, which, duly mounted in an enormous chassis, received the revered Zeppelin appellation.

■ The Maybach W6 featured on these pages—its Spohn-built body resting on a 144-inch wheelbase—is identical to the mighty Zeppelin in every aspect, except that its hood hides a straight six, a detail that cut the Zeppelin's chassis-only price of $8000 in half. Bore and stroke of the 7.0-liter (427-cubic-inch) unit is 94 mm by 168, with an output of 120 hp at 2200 rpm. ■ The W6 range was offered between 1930 and 1937; some 100 were built, but only three copies of the cabriolet bodystyle featured in the Collection are known to have survived. Two decades of Maybach production, from 1921 to 1941, resulted in approximately 2300 examples—just enough to sustain its exclusivity.

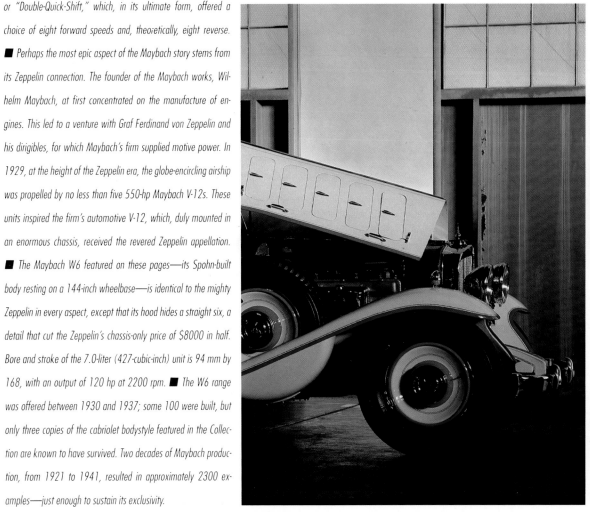

STUTZ

MODEL DV-32 VICTORIA

■ Stutz holds a special place among American classics, one earned not only through its advanced engineering and its racing successes, but also through its image, which was burnished with a certain European flair. ■ Born in 1876 on an Ohio farm, Harry Clayton Stutz soon left the rural ways of his Dutch parents for bustling Dayton. Years filled with a variety of ventures followed, but by 1910 he had moved on to Indianapolis, where he built a potent racer. Entered in the 1911 inaugural of the 500-mile race, the Stutz finished in eleventh place—not bad for a debutant.

■ When Stutz began building replicas of his Indianapolis car, its racing roots were recalled with the famous slogan "The Car That Made Good in a Day." In another linguistic coup, Stutz called his roadster "Bearcat"—a catchy name for a hairy machine of true sports car heritage. ■ The company initiated public trading of its stock in 1915, a venture that drove Harry Stutz out of the firm in 1919 when manipulator Alan Ryan bought control of the company, culminating in a debacle remembered on Wall Street as the "Stutz Corner." Harry Stutz went on to fame as a builder of fire trucks, but died prematurely in 1930. ■ The Twenties saw Stutz adrift—a tack broken by the arrival of Frederick Moskovics, the Hungarian emigré of Marmon fame, who charted a new course by charging Charles Greuter, a Swiss-born engineer, with the task of creating an

eight-cylinder engine that would emulate the single-overhead-cam tradition of Europe's famed Alfas and Hispanos. Wrapped in an ever-increasing variety of coachwork—twenty-eight bodystyles were offered in 1928—the Vertical Eight brought both sales—a record production of 5000 in 1926—and racing successes—a sensational second at Le Mans in 1928. ■ By 1931, the multicylinder war forced Stutz, whose Depression-ravaged coffers could not afford a new engine, to creative exploitation of its existing straight-eight. The DV-32—named for its valvetrain—sounded aggressively advanced, even superior, when compared to the competition's V-12s and V-16s. Sporting double overhead cams and hemispherical combustion chambers, the DV-32's bore and stroke of 3.4 inches by 4.5 created a displacement of 322 cubic inches (5.2 liters) and an output of 156 hp at 3900 rpm. Mounted in the Bearcat—a name revived for a shorter, 135-inch-wheelbase model—the engine produced a top speed of over 100 mph. ■ The Collection's DV-32—its 145-inch chassis supporting an exquisite Rollston body costing $7400—spent its postwar years under a bridge in the Bronx, parked there by a GI who never returned. ■ Despite Stutz's avant-garde image, production, by 1933, had dwindled to 110 units. The following year, with only six cars assembled, marked the final demise of once-proud Stutz.

BUGATTI

TYPE 57 AERODYNAMIQUE

■ With an address like "Automobiles E. Bugatti, Molsheim, Bas-Rhin, Alsace," the exotic nature of the product originating from this village in Northern France was established right at the doorstep. Further marvels met the visitor as he proceeded beyond the gates. ■ Not only had Ettore Bugatti built an impressive factory in Alsace-Lorraine, close to the German border, but also vineyards, riding stables and even an inn where customers were accommodated in grand style; through all that surrounded "Le Patron" had to flow "Le Pur Sang"—the pure blood. ■ Born in Milan, Italy, in 1881, Ettore Bugatti was raised by a family of artists— no wonder that the cars he set out to build in 1909 were works of art. The next two decades saw a stream of masterpieces emerge from Molsheim. Foremost among them were such classics as the Type 35, a dominant force on the Grand Prix circuits of the day, and the Type 41—"La Royale"—with its unsurpassed magnificence. ■ By the mid-Thirties, the idyllic tranquility of Molsheim had been exchanged for an atmosphere of confrontation. Nationwide worker unrest had reached the region, and "Le Patron" had fled to Paris in bitter disappointment. The Type 57, which was to embody the best of fast long-distance motoring, had barely been completed. It was up to Ettore's son, Jean, to continue the work. The son proved no less an artist than the father, and, even though some of the

Bugatti's endearing mechanical eccentricity wilted away under Jean's regime, the beauty of his creations have given them a special stature. ■ The Collection's Type 57 represents the more sedate aspects of Jean's production but still illustrates the unique line that flew from his pen. Its two-door, four-seat body was built at Molsheim, as were most of the closed Type 57 bodies. ■ The straight-eight, double overhead-cam engine that powers this Type 57 has a bore and stroke of 72 mm by 100, a displacement of 3.3 liters (200 cubic inches) and an output of 140 hp at 4800 rpm— producing a top speed of around 100 mph. Its 130-inch wheelbase chassis weighs 2100 pounds. ■ In contrast to previous Bugatti practice, the Type 57 had its four-speed, constant-mesh gearbox mounted at the rear of the engine—no longer in unit with the rear axle. Less than 710 were built of the various Type 57 versions, which later included the 57C, 57S and the 57SC. ■ The Type 57 remained in production until 1939, when Jean, swerving to avoid a drunken bicyclist, was killed during the testing of a racer. Later, the factory was taken over by the Germans; the hallowed halls that once housed exotic cars were now subverted to the manufacture of amphibious vehicles and torpedoes. ■ After the war, Ettore attempted to launch the Type 73, but the project died with the death of "Le Patron" in 1947.

BUICK

SERIES 90 TOWN CAR

■ Among Charles S. Howard's nicknames was "Rough Rider Charley," bestowed on him after he charged up San Juan Hill with Teddy Roosevelt. It stuck when he began a career in automobile racing that took him to victory in numerous events. Howard had good luck with the horses, too, campaigning a filly named Sea Biscuit that became the top money winner of its era. But what Charley Howard enjoyed more than anything else was selling Buicks. ■ It was none other than William Crapo Durant who lured Howard into the Buick business. Eager to expand the line, Durant dispatched Howard around the country to set up dealerships. ■ The cars he promoted were given their name by David Dunbar Buick in 1903. Buick had ventured into automobiles after inventing a process for applying porcelain to cast iron, giving the world a better bathtub. His initial prototype may have been completed as early as 1899, but the real news came in 1903 when Buick Engineer Eugene Richard patented America's first valve-in-head engine. Getting Buicks into production was another matter, however, and it took three tries before Buick found a backer, one Billy Durant. ■ David Buick would be forced out of his firm by 1908, but Durant steamed forward, thanks to true believers like Charley Howard, who settled in San Francisco in 1905 with a Buick franchise of his own. By 1912, Howard was responsible for selling Buicks throughout most of the

western U.S. and earned the new nickname of "Train Load Charley" after filling an entire train with Buicks destined for eager West Coast buyers. ■ Buick's California sales peaked in 1927 and began a downhill slide that would see demand sink to 3200 cars by 1932. But it didn't stop Howard from presenting his wife Anita with a 1931 Buick carrying an elegant town car body by Murphy, California's most innovative coachbuilder. ■ Its wood-framed aluminum body was almost identical to contemporary Duesenberg designs, with a rakishly angled windshield, rectangular side windows and polished aluminum trim. The chassis on which it rolled was based on the division's 90 Series, its wheelbase stretched to 138 inches for the new coachwork. ■ Buick went "all-Eight" in 1931, and the 90 Series cars initially used an overhead-valve straight eight with a bore and stroke of 3.3 inches by 5.0, for a total displacement of 345 cubic inches (5.6 liters) and an output of 104 hp at 2800 rpm. The following year, Howard replaced the original chassis with a 1932 version equipped with a newly optional high-compression 113-hp eight. ■ The Murphy Buick was long thought to have belonged to Bing Crosby because the crooner was often seen with it at horse tracks around California. But it was in fact an elegant testimony to Charlie Howard's tireless enthusiasm for his product, a Buick man to the end.

CORD

MODEL 812 PHAETON

■ On a clear day in the fall of 1940, workers along the road from Tucson to Phoenix suddenly became aware of a plume of dust in the distance. There was nothing unusual about that—the road was just a trail of packed sand in those days—but this time, as the cloud came closer, its vortex approaching at a breakneck speed, the car did not slow down. ■ As the crew scrambled to safety, the yellow monster smashed through the barriers at the work site. Swerving wildly, the car plowed headlong into the ditch the workers had been digging, overturned and crushed its driver. Tom Mix, hero of the silver screen, lay dead at the age of 60. ■ Today, the monument that marks the spot of Mix's demise also serves as an epitaph of sorts for the car he was driving, a Cord 812, which had met its own demise three years earlier. ■ The seed that grew into the 810 Cord had been sown by Gordon Buehrig in sketches dated November 7, 1933. Here his fertile mind had formulated plans for a futuristic automobile, with a sealed engine compartment flanked by outrigger radiators that snuggled between separate pontoon fenders. ■ The 810 had been conceived as a "baby Duesenberg," but Buehrig's work on the Auburn Boattail Speedster placed the project in limbo. Back on the board, Buehrig refined his sketches into a patent drawing, which was registered on October 2, 1934. ■ The on-again off-

again project received the go-ahead in July of 1935. Its introduction was set for November 2 at the New York Auto Show, which left less than four months to develop a prototype and build 100 examples. Against all odds, the task was accomplished, but—thanks to the cars having been built by hand—the cost grew so high that it spelled the beginning of the end. ■ Mechanically, the 810 Cord was inspired by its front-wheel-drive predecessor, the L-29. This time the engine was a 90-degree V-8, designed for Cord by Lycoming's Forest Baster. Bore and stroke measured 3.5 inches by 3.8, for a displacement of 289 cubic inches (4.7 liters) and an output of 125 hp at 3500 rpm. Its four-speed transmission, featuring electro-vacuum activated gear selection via a lever on the steering column, was located ahead of the engine. The 810's wheelbase was 125 inches, weight 3650 pounds and top speed 90 mph. Available originally in four bodystyles starting at $1995, the 810 was superseded in 1937 by the $2445 812, whose optional supercharger increased output to 170 hp and top speed to 110 mph. ■ The Cord featured in the Collection is the actual car in which Tom Mix met his maker. It was sold wrecked to R. E. Nelson on October 3, 1942 for $100. Restored, it still features Mix's gun holster, as well as his oversized gas pedal, which he unfortunately had a habit of keeping pressed to the floor.

■ AMERICA'S FAVORITE COWBOY WAS KILLED BY HIS OWN CORD

CHRYSLER

CUSTOM IMPERIAL EIGHT PHAETON

There was a time, at the dawn of the automotive century, when a man with a bright idea could start with two empty hands and end up owning an empire. But as the market swelled and economic Darwinism weeded out weak organizations, leaving only the strong, the strong grew very strong. Building a company from scratch soon became impossible. ■ Against this backdrop, Walter Percy Chrysler and the empire he launched in 1924 must be regarded as Detroit's last great success story. Born in 1875, in Wamego, Kansas, Chrysler went from sweeping Union Pacific Railroad roundhouses to a millionaire as general manager of Buick in just twenty years. ■ After all this, a scrap with GM boss Billy Durant in 1920 sent Chrysler looking for a job, which he soon found—at a salary of a cool million a year. His assignment was to make Willys-Overland profitable, which he did. But all this was before his real success story had even begun. ■ On his way up, Chrysler had assembled a brilliant trio of engineers: Carl Breer, Fred Zeder and Owen Skelton—"The Three Musketeers" as Chrysler called them. This team was set to design a car that would be the first to carry the Chrysler name. Introduced at Manhattan's Commodore Hotel in 1924, the new car was a smash hit. Production went from 32,000 in 1925 to 162,000 in 1926. ■ The model most eloquently illustrating Chrysler's formula for success—a

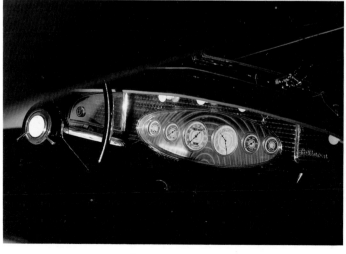

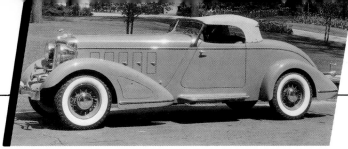

■ A LE BARON CUSTOM FOR A CHRYSLER SON

great deal of value for not a whole lot of money—arrived in 1927 with the introduction of a prestige line named Imperial. The Collection's example—a 1933 Le Baron-built dual-cowl CL Phaeton that originally cost $3395 and was replicated only thirty-six times—is one of the finest. ■ Power came from an L-head straight-eight engine, featuring a bore and stroke of 3.5 inches by 5.0, a displacement of 385 cubic inches (6.3 liters) and a choice of 125 hp or 135 hp outputs at 3200 rpm. The manual transmission was a four-speed unit. Four-wheel Lockheed hydraulic brakes were standard and the wheelbase measured 146 inches. ■ Chrysler's Imperial was always ranked a notch below the greatest of the classics. And perhaps this was justified—from a mechanical viewpoint, certainly—as the Chrysler engine never approached the sophistication of those from Duesenberg or Stutz. On the other hand, the styling of the Imperial's semi-custom bodies—especially the beautiful example seen here with its sloping radiator, vee-shaped headlights and sweeping hood and fenders—rivals the best of the classics. ■ Walter Chrysler retired in 1935. While still at the helm he had presided over that great fiasco, the Airflow, for which he must be forgiven. It was, after all, a brilliant concept—too brilliant for the times. The founder died in 1940, and thus lived to see Chrysler back on track, ready and able to take on the road that lay ahead.

MERCEDES-BENZ

TYP G4 GELANDEWAGEN

■ In the early Thirties, as the Third Reich was cranking up its war machinery, a number of German concerns saw an increasing share of their capacity devoted to military production. The most prestigious of the automakers, Daimler-Benz, was no exception. ■ In 1934, the company unveiled a remarkable six-wheeler designated G4. The "G" stood for "gelände," German for cross-country. The vehicle was intended for command use, but experience in the field revealed that its excessive weight—well over 8000 pounds—made its fitness for this type of work questionable—despite the added traction of its four rugged rear wheels. Instead, the G4's primary role became that of a parade vehicle for party dignitaries. ■ Regardless of its utilization, the G4 represented automotive engineering at its best. It was built in the mold of the contemporary Grosser Mercedes, but used the 5.0-liter (305-cubic-inch) engine from the 500K, later updated to the 540K's 5.4-liter (330-cubic-inch) motor. In the latter configuration, the overhead-valve, straight-eight produced 115 hp at 2000 rpm. ■ Because of the G4's original mandate as an off-road vehicle, it did not share the 500/540K's on-demand supercharger. Coupled to a suitably geared four-speed transmission—equipped with two reverse ratios—the engine generated a top speed of 50 mph. Up front the 160-inch-wheelbase chassis displayed standard Mercedes fare,

while in the rear, rigid axles replaced swing axles. ■ If the engineers went all out, so did the coachbuilders. Seating was for seven; two up front, two on folding chairs in the middle, and three on a rear bench. Sumptuous leather covered all surfaces. Leather was also used in the trunk, where the occupants could stow their belongings in fitted luggage. ■ A total of 57 units were built between 1934 and 1939. One of the last G4s was presented to Generalissimo Franco and still remains with the Spanish state. Only three additional examples are known to have survived. ■ The G4 acquired by the Collection was delivered to the German Army High Command on September 6, 1938, as duly noted on a factory document. A curious addendum suggests that the vehicle might have been diverted to the personal use of Mussolini; it seems the G4 was transported to Genoa on August 27, 1939, for further shipment to Tripoli, Libya—then under Italian occupation. ■ The tracks made by the G4 as it found its way to Los Angeles after the war have long since been obliterated. For many years it belonged to Pacific Auto Rental, a company supplying vehicles to the movie industry. In this capacity, it played many a starring role, including an appearance in the television series "Hogan's Heroes." ■ It was subsequently restored to its original splendor by the craftsmen of the Collection's own restoration shop.

■ THE GARGANTUAN G4 WAS OFTEN UNDONE BY ITS OWN WEIGHT

DUESENBERG

MODEL J TOWN CAR

■ In 1878, in the town of Lippe, Germany, the Duesenbergs welcomed a new addition to their family—a son, christened Frederic. A year later, another son arrived; he would be called August. Seven years later, inspired by glowing reports from the New World, the family emigrated to America. ■ By the time they reached their nineteenth and twentieth birthdays, the Duesenberg brothers had distinguished themselves by building and racing bicycles. In 1898, for example, Fred set a world record over the two-mile distance. It was only natural that the brothers would choose to manufacture bicycles of their own, but their first venture, established in Des Moines, succumbed to bankruptcy in 1903. ■ The brothers remained in Des Moines, and it was here, in 1904, that they built their first automobile, the robust and racy two-cylinder Mason. It took another few years before they reached the Brickyard, but their improved four-cylinder Mason failed to qualify. ■ A decade later, the picture was dramatically different. In 1913, the Duesenbergs founded their own firm, and in 1921, Jimmy Murphy drove a straight-eight Duesenberg to victory in the French Grand Prix. The Duesenberg went on to become one of the most famous racing machines of the era, winning the Indianapolis 500 in 1924, 1925 and 1927. ■ A road car, the Model A, had been introduced in 1920, but its drowsy bodywork made it a slow seller, and by

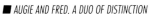
■ AUGIE AND FRED, A DUO OF DISTINCTION

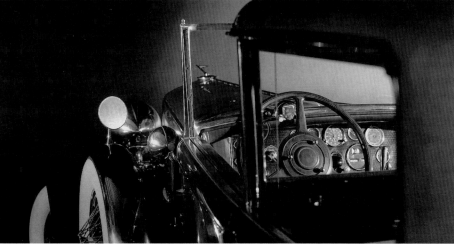

1927 the brothers were once again in trouble—only to be saved by E. L. Cord. ■ The Cord era brought Duesenberg into the company of the world's greatest cars thanks to the engineering genius of Fred Duesenberg, the styling talent of Gordon Buehrig and the financial savvy of Errett Lobban Cord. ■ The crown jewel of the Duesenberg chassis was its Lycoming-built, double-overhead-cam, 32-valve, straight-eight engine, producing 265 hp at 4200 rpm. Bore and stroke measured 3.8 inches by 4.8, for a displacement of 420 cubic inches (6.9 liters). A speed of 90 mph could be reached in the middle gear of the three-speed transmission, with a top speed of 116 mph. The chassis came in two wheelbase configurations, 143 and 154 inches. ■ The Model J shown here is an outstanding example of a Murphy town car built on the 154-inch chassis, one of twelve from ʻthe Pasadena, California, firm. With 32,000 miles on the odometer, the car is still completely original, right down to the paint, and is believed to be the most pristine example in existence. Its original owner was band leader Paul Whiteman. ■ In 1937, beset by financial problems, Cord sold his empire, effectively killing the Duesenberg. Its demise was not seen by Fred, however, who five years earlier, at the age of 54, never recovered from an accident in one of his own cars. Thus ended the career of one of the greatest names in automotive engineering.

PACKARD

MODEL 1605 SUPER EIGHT

■ Packard, unlike so many of its colleagues, managed to weather the Depression—but not without a tarnished image. Financial survival had meant giving up some of the exclusivity that had built its enviable image. ■ In 1932, alarmed by dwindling sales, Packard introduced the Light-Eight, an "economy car." It failed to attract the desired customers, however, and was discontinued the same year. The 120, announced in 1935, was another attempt at a lower-priced model, and this time the approach succeeded. By 1937, when the 120 reached the market in full force, annual production soared to a record level of nearly 50,000 units. ■ For 1938, the Packard line consisted of the Six, the Eight, the Super Eight and, at the top of the ladder, the Twelve. It was an orderly hierarchy that spanned the spectrum from relative economy, with prices beginning at $975 for a Six Business Coupe, to definitive extravagance, with $8510 for a V-12 Touring Cabriolet by Brunn. ■ Regardless of its flirtation with the masses, Packard remained a favorite with the upper crust—a fact underscored by the many rich and famous who chose Packards for their transportation. Not only was the leader of the free world, Franklin Delano Roosevelt, partial to America's premier luxury car, but dictators in particular seemed to have a propensity for Packards, as illustrated by Stalin's Super Eight Convertible Sedan, and by the Collection's Super Eight—a

dual-cowl Phaeton bodied by the Rosemont, Pennsylvania firm of Derham—was previously owned by Argentine strongman Juan Perón. ■ Compared to the angular styling of the early Thirties, the look of the late Thirties was characterized by smoothly streamlined fenders and all-enveloping bodies. Packard followed the trend, but slowly. Its headlights, for instance, were still mounted on the exterior, in the classic mode—although they had now taken on the fashionable teardrop shape. A further concession to the aerodynamic vogue was the introduction of a vee-shaped windshield. ■ The Super Eight received its power from Packard's familiar straight-eight, now with a bore and stroke of 3.2 inches by 5.0, a displacement of 320 cubic inches (5.2 liters) and an output of 130 hp at 3200 rpm—a powerplant giving smooth and effortless propulsion at any speed. Its refinement was further enhanced by a selective-synchromesh three-speed transmission. The Super Eight's ride was already smooth, but improved further with a semi-floating rear axle. The weight of the Derham Phaeton—resting on a 151-inch wheelbase—was around 5000 pounds and the price in the $10,000 range. ■ The next two decades saw Packard decline steadily towards its regrettable extinction. During the late Thirties—in the last throes of the classic era—however, the top-of-the-line Packards revealed few signs of fading glory.

TYP 540K CABRIOLET B

■ Nineteen thirty-six marked the golden anniversary of Mercedes-Benz. The previous year, Mercedes had completely dominated the Grand Prix scene, a feat accompanied by an understandable increase in public prestige. More of the same was expected for 1936—especially because of the anniversary. The Porsche-designed "silver arrows" of the Auto-Union team, however, would have none of that. Rudolf Caracciola did manage to nudge his Mercedes to wins in Monaco and Tunis, but this amounted to nothing compared to Auto Union's Bernd Rosemeyer and his fabulous string of victories. ■ If fame and fortune eluded Mercedes on the track in 1936, conditions on the road, however, appeared most encouraging: At that year's Berlin show, the Stuttgart firm introduced the latest installment in its continuing saga of Autobahn champions—the 540K. ■ This model differed only slightly from its predecessor, the 500K; its enlarged cylinders, now measuring 88 mm by 111, translated into a displacement of 5.4 liters (332 cubic inches). Output—the point of the exercise, after all—improved concomitantly, to 115 hp at 3400 rpm and 180 hp with the supercharger engaged—a gain of 15 hp and 20 hp respectively over the 500K. A slight increase in speed translated to a new maximum velocity of just over 100 mph. Chassiswise, the 540K remained unchanged, retaining its 131.5-inch wheelbase and its 5160-

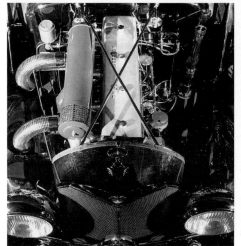

pound weight. The four-speed transmission remained as well, although it was joined in late 1939 by a five-speed version. ■ In the engineering department, the sudden death of Hans Nibel in 1934 had propelled Max Sailer to the post of chief engineer. His associate in charge of passenger car design, and the father of the 540K, was Hans-Gustav Rohr. A year after the introduction of his favorite son, Rohr, aged 42, also died suddenly. ■ In the styling department, Hermann Ahrens continued to evolve the stunning look that had become a Mercedes hallmark. Starting in 1938, for example, 540Ks received new front fenders that more fully enveloped the front wheels. Another change advanced the radiator from its original position behind the front axle to one right above it. This was not accompanied by a longer hood, however, as the change was used to increase interior room. ■ Altogether, approximately 406 540Ks were built at Mercedes' Sindelfingen coachworks between 1936 and 1939. The car featured here, a 1938 Cabriolet B originally delivered to an English customer, is one of 95 540Ks built that year. ■ Performance and exclusivity, combined with styling that expressed elegance without excess, made the 540K a winner. Regardless of venue—Cannes, Budapest or Villars—the Mercedes was a sure bet in any concours d'élégance. Time has only added to its eminence.

GRAHAM

MODEL 97 FOUR-DOOR SEDAN

■ After a spectacular rise to prominence in the late Twenties, when annual production hit a high of 73,000 units, the post-Crash Thirties found Graham in need of a shot in the arm. Styling and supercharging were the potions expected to do the trick. While, in the end, neither had the desired effect, the effort produced a memorable product. ■ The Graham had its roots in a company called Paige-Detroit, founded in 1909. By the outbreak of World War I, "Detroit" had been dropped, and the Paige name alone adorned a range of new designs. ■ In 1927, the company was taken over by the Graham brothers, who had made their mark and their money in a joint venture with another brother team, the Dodges. The Paige badge now received the addition of the Graham name, becoming the Graham-Paige. By 1930 the Paige portion was dropped. ■ Graham's supercharger was introduced in 1934—a first for a moderately-priced car—and made the straight-eight Blue Streak worthy of its name; top speed was in the 95 mph range. As with the Duesenberg supercharger, the Graham version was of the centrifugal type and improved mid-range performance. ■ Although production had risen from a low of 11,000 in 1933 to 21,000 in 1937, the Graham brothers were not satisfied. They returned to Amos Northup, who had been responsible for the styling of the Blue Streak. Northup came through

with an extraordinary effort, christened the "Sharknose." While Gordon Buehrig's ground-breaking design for the 810 Cord—which itself was nicknamed the "Coffin Nose"—adhered to the principle of "form follows function," Northup's design drew its inspiration from trends in the decorative arts. ■ Introduced in 1938, the Sharknose was available only as a four-door sedan; Model 96 was unsupercharged, Model 97 supercharged, the latter priced from $1198. Under the skin, the frame was redesigned to allow a lower profile, although the engine was essentially unchanged: an L-head six with a bore and stroke of 3.3 inches by 4.4, and a displacement of 218 cubic inches (3.6 liters). Output for the supercharged version was 120 hp, which propelled the 3300-pound car to 60 mph in 16 seconds. Its four-speed transmission incorporated a fuel-saving overdrive. ■ Although an aesthetic triumph, the Sharknose did not go over well with the public; the Graham organization dipped into the red. While further desperate efforts at recovery were made, the last automotive breath had been drawn by 1940. With the war, the factory turned to military production. ■ Today, the Sharknose cuts a startling figure on the Collection floor, where its radical front end—perhaps the most extreme of the Art Deco era—has earned it the same prominent place it holds in the annals of automotive design.

CADILLAC

■ The far-reaching effects of the Crash slowly began to ebb by the late Thirties. Yet though the economy was on the upswing and Americans were returning to work, the opulence that had reached its zenith just as the market was reaching its nadir would never be seen again. ■ As the Depression spiraled downward, it took most of the great marques with it: Duesenberg, Cord and Auburn were gone by 1937, as were Marmon and Peerless. And Packard was mortally wounded by the time its production lines were turned over to building PT boat engines. Only Cadillac and Lincoln would survive the war in fighting trim. ■ In February 1933, Cadillac President Lawrence P. Fisher announced that V-16 production would be limited to 400 cars that year, but the bad times called his bluff and only 338 emerged between 1933 and 1937. ■ The original Cadillac V-16 was a jewel-like powerplant befitting "The Standard of the World," but it was also one of the most complex, incorporating some 3300 parts. When Nicholas Dreystadt, formerly Cadillac's general manager of parts and service, took over from Fisher in 1934, he knew the importance of the V-16 to Cadillac's exclusivity—but he also knew the cost of its complexity. ■ One way to simplify it was to take advantage of the manufacturing techniques developed for Cadillac's 1936 V-8 that allowed the crankcase and cylinder block to be cast as a single unit. Another was to eliminate

the separate intake manifolds and carburetors by spreading the angle of the cylinder banks from 45 degrees to an unprecedented 135, allowing for a single manifold to be inserted between them while maintaining an angle that would deliver Cadillac's characteristic smoothness. In addition to using fewer parts, the new engine's stroke was reduced to 3.3 inches, while its bore was enlarged to the same distance. The result was a minor decrease in displacement from 452 cubic inches to 431 (7.1 liters) but a weight savings of 250 pounds. Output was largely unchanged, 185 bhp at 3800 rpm. ■ It would not be until 1940 that W.C. Fields would team with Mae West for the film "My Little Chickadee," but the two already had something in common in 1938: an appreciation for the new Cadillac Sixteens that went on sale in October 1937. Miss West made hers a seven-passenger formal sedan, but Fields would buy two: a two-door coupe and the seven-passenger sedan seen here that was later acquired by the Collection. Fields, well-known for his like of liquid refreshment, installed bars in both, with an electric martini mixer in the latter. ■ As with all other Sixteens that year, both cars rode on 141-inch wheelbases. Prices started at $5100 and climbed as high as $7200, small change for a man who so mistrusted banks that he deposited his generous earnings in over 700 accounts around the country.

DELAHAYE

TYPE 175S AERODYNAMIQUE

■ Spanning half a tumultuous century, the Delahaye story represents legend-building on a grand scale. At the introduction of the epic appears Emile Delahaye, an engineer from Tours, France, whose place among the pioneers was secured by virtue of the automobile he built in 1895. ■ Despite his pioneering role, Delahaye, who died in 1905, never became the grand master of his own marque. That title belongs to Charles Weiffenbach, known among his peers as Monsieur Charles. Joining the firm at the turn of the century, he remained at the helm until Delahaye closed its doors in 1954. ■ Over the years, Monsieur Charles expanded the Delahaye name to represent not only an armada of passenger cars, but also trucks and fire engines. In the early Thirties, however, the creative spirit seemed to have left him; Delahayes lost their distinctive edge, sending the fortunes of the marque into a tailspin.

■ Then, in 1933, inspired it is said by Ettore Bugatti, Weiffenbach launched a breathtaking crop of high-performance machines. The following year, a Delahaye broke seven world records at Montlhéry. Further victories secured soaring sales and renewed prosperity. Adding to the Delahaye grandeur during this period were the fabulous bodies bestowed on them by France's most famous coachbuilders, Figoni et Falaschi foremost among them.

■ Giuseppe Figoni, an Italian, had arrived in Paris with his parents

at the turn of the century. After serving his apprenticeship in a wagon builder's shop, the young man soon set up his own coachbuilding works in the fashionable suburb of Boulogne-Sur-Seine. By 1935, Figoni—the artist—had acquired a style that set automobile enthusiasts on fire. He had also acquired a partner, fellow Italian Ovidio Falaschi—the businessman. ■ The five-seat Delahaye seen on these pages is the prototype of Monseiur Charles' first postwar model and an outstanding example of Figoni at his best. In addition to its flowing lines—the aerodynamic appearance based more on artistic interpretation than empirical research—the design features a remarkably futuristic removable glass roof. ■ Below the seductive skin hides a 4.5-liter (275-cubic-inch), 140-hp straight-six with a bore and stroke of 94 mm by 107. The 132-inch wheelbase chassis rests on Dubonnet independent suspension up front and a de Dion axle at the rear. The four-speed transmission features the Cotal semi-automatic preselector system. ■ Restored to perfection, this one-off Delahaye represents the zenith of the coachbuilder's craft—and the end of an era. The cost of handcraftsmanship had climbed too high in an age of mass production. By 1951, the Type 175 had been replaced by the Type 235, a model that lacked the excitement of the past and failed to stem the company's slide towards its 1954 extinction.

MAYBACH

TYP SW38 CABRIOLET

Maybach, through its founder Wilhelm Maybach, benefited from a prestigious association with one of the world's earliest automotive efforts, Gottlieb Daimler's 1886 motor carriage, the result of a collaboration between Daimler and Maybach. ■ Born in Heilbronn, Germany, in 1846, Maybach was, by age twenty-six, the chief engineer of the Gasmotorenfabrik Deutz, a pioneer in the field of gasoline engines. The person doing the hiring was none other than Gottlieb Daimler. The wives of the two men had been friends since school days, a circumstance that, coupled with the professional collaboration between their husbands, fostered a close relationship—one that would lead to their collaboration and last until Daimler's death in 1900. ■ World War I found Maybach, now joined by his son Karl, producing motive power for the airborne war effort. After the war, forbidden to manufacture aero engines, the Maybachs switched to automobiles—a move resulting in the 1920 introduction of the W2. ■ The next few years saw a production of about 700 units, which included the W5, introduced in 1926. The year of Wilhelm's death, 1929, marked the arrival of Maybach's "tour de force," the fabulous V-12 Zeppelin—of which the Collection owns an unrestored example. In 1930, broadening its commercial base, Maybach brought out the W6, a design identical to that of the Zeppelin's, but powered by a six-cylinder engine.

In 1935 appeared another Maybach classic, the all-new SW35, sporting a six-cylinder engine and rolling on an advanced chassis featuring independent suspension up front and swing axles at the rear. Its SW designation was derived from "Schwingachse," German for swing axle. ■ The engine was enlarged in 1936, creating the SW38—an example of which is seen on these pages. Its body rests on a 134-inch wheelbase, and was built by Spohn, the foremost supplier of Maybach coachwork. ■ The SW38's single-overhead-cam engine, producing 140 hp at 4000 rpm, had a bore and stroke of 90 mm by 100 and a displacement of 3.8 liters (233 cubic inches). The transmission featured the intricate "Doppelschnellgang" system, which gave a choice of eight forward gears. Top speed was around 90 mph. ■ Another displacement increase in 1939 created the SW42. Maybach continued production until 1941, when, among other military machinery, a 700 hp V-12 was built—a unit used in Porsche's famous Tiger tank. Two decades of civilian production resulted in some 2300 cars, approximately one-half of which were the SW-type. ■ Sometimes called Germany's Rolls-Royce, Maybach lived up to this appellation as far as quality and prestige were concerned. It even surpassed its British counterpart when it came to engineering refinement. As for exclusivity, there was simply no comparison.

TUCKER

MODEL 48 FOUR-DOOR SEDAN

More than any other automobile, the Tucker represents the entrepreneurial free-for-all of early postwar America. Even before Preston Tucker and his car became heroes of the big screen, there were many whose emotions stirred at the recollection of the super-promoter introducing "The First New Car in Fifty Years." ■ Perhaps, if being a bully has something to do with bullishness, Tucker's background as both a car salesman and a policeman might explain the aggressiveness with which he pursued his goals.

■ Tucker's first automotive effort involved Harry Miller, with whom he developed plans for a rear-engined sports car called the Torpedo. Although the project was abandoned, out of it grew greater ambitions. Tucker now wanted to build a car for the masses, an automobile so advanced it would knock the breath out of both the public and the established manufacturers. ■ Tucker turned to stylist Alex Tremulis, who, expanding on the Torpedo, created a new design in one week. Sketches in hand, Tucker proceeded to raise capital through a stock issue that attracted 44,000 shareholders. He also signed up dealers, leased production facilities and even went as far as selling accessory kits—for cars that didn't yet exist. ■ The fact that nothing more than a prototype had been built soon became a source of dubious speculation; a 100-day crash program produced fifty examples. Displayed around the

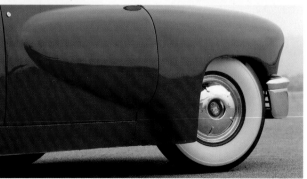

country, these pilots provided tangible proof that the Tucker was indeed the most advanced car of its time. ■ The streamlined body featured three headlights, the center "Cyclops" lamp turning with the wheels for safer operation at night. A host of other safety features included a windshield that popped out on impact. Below the space-age surface, the 4235-pound car sported all-independent suspension on a 128-inch wheelbase. The transmission was a vacuum-operated, four-speed manual unit, but production cars were to receive an automatic version. ■ The rear-mounted engine was a flat, opposed six, developed for helicopter use by Air-Cooled Motors. The overhead-valve, oversquare unit—converted to water cooling—had a bore and stroke of 4.5 inches by 3.5, a displacement of 334 cubic inches (5.5 liters) and an output of 166 hp at 3200 rpm. Top speed was 110 mph. And it could be yours for $2450. ■ But then the Federal watchdogs entered the act. Charged with securities violations, Tucker was indicted for fraud. His trial ended in acquittal, but by then the momentum was lost. Tucker sought vindication in his book "My Car Was Too Good." Perhaps, with time, it could have been good. Burdened by a 58 percent rear bias, however, it is doubtful that the handling could ever have become acceptable. ■ As a collector car the Tucker has shown remarkable longevity; of the 51 built, 49 remain.

■ PRESTON TUCKER IN A PROMOTIONAL POSE

BANTAM

MODEL 60 DE LUXE ROADSTER

■ The Bantam story begins with Britain's Austin Seven, Sir Herbert Austin's brainchild, the world's first mass-produced small car. Introduced in 1922, this lovable creature stayed in production for sixteen years and was reproduced a quarter of a million times. ■ It is said that imitation is the truest form of flattery—in Germany the Seven became the Dixi, in France the Rosengart, and in Japan it saw unapproved reincarnation as a Datsun. ■ With a vision of his creation conquering the world, Sir Herbert traveled to New York in January 1929. He returned with a production agreement, and the first cars appeared in the spring of 1930, built by the American Austin Car Company of Butler, Pennsylvania. Although Austin under the skin, the American version had been restyled by Alexis de Sakhnoffsky, who performed wonders with its small proportions, even giving the roadster model a fancy Duesenberg-like sweep panel. ■ The Crash had hit during the fall of 1929, but Austin remained optimistic. With hard times on the horizon, they were confident of their timing. The bitter reality soon became clear, however—a mere 8558 units found buyers in 1930, and the factory doors closed in early 1932. They did not open until the arrival of super-salesman Roy Evans, whose efforts led to an additional 10,000 units. This was still not enough—the doors closed again in 1934. ■ It seemed that a vehicle taken seri-

ously in England and elsewhere had turned into a joke on the other side of the Atlantic. The toy-like cars earned a smile whenever seen —although not on the lips of owners who sometimes had trouble finding their cars when pranksters moved them to the most improbable spots. ■ Evans tried again in 1938. With Sakhnoffsky performing his magic once more, the car—updated under the skin as well—hit the showrooms as the Bantam, its badge sporting the image of a proud rooster. Its four-cylinder engine had a bore and stroke of 2.3 inches by 3.1, a displacement of 50 cubic inches (0.81 liters) and an output of 22 hp at 3800 rpm. Top speed and fuel consumption were claimed to be 60—mph and mpg respectively. Wheelbase was 75 inches and weight 1200 pounds. Priced from $399 to $565, the Bantam seemed a bargain, but Americans didn't care. Total sales for 1938, 1939 and 1940 were just over 4000 units, with a final 138 unloaded in 1941. ■ Evans struck pay dirt when the military chose a Bantam-built prototype to become the Jeep—a vehicle of which the firm built few examples, although it did lead to other military contracts. ■ In the end, like a boxer saved by the bell, Bantam, the company, had been saved by the war. Bantam, the car, however, could not be saved. After the war, its dies and jigs were never found. And that was just as well. Soon, a bug would accomplish what the rooster never could.

MUNTZ

JET CONVERTIBLE COUPE

■ Nothing stirs the appetite quite as much as having to do without. The Thirties and Forties robbed a generation of its right to pursuit of prosperity; the Depression, leaving lurid snapshots of misery, was followed by the attack on Pearl Harbor, forcing the nation into yet another period of denial. By 1945, Americans were desperate for the trappings of affluence. ■ Nothing embodies the good life quite as much as the automobile, and soon makers were scrambling to meet the pent-up demand. In this climate, two talented men—an engineer and a salesman—both operating out of Glendale, California, would make names for themselves. ■ Frank Kurtis, the engineer, was already a successful manufacturer of midget racers. In 1948, he turned to another project, a sporty two-seater. Built from off-the-shelf components, the Kurtis was nothing more than an assembled car—and an expensive one at that. Only some thirty-six were built during 1948 and 1949. ■ Earl Muntz, the salesman, was a prodigy. At the age of eight, he assembled and sold radios. At twenty, he owned a used-car lot in Elgin, Illinois. Soon, booming Southern California beckoned. There, back in the used-car business, "Madman Muntz"—aided by outrageous radio commercials—earned both a fortune and a nickname. In 1947, entering the big league, he launched his own brand of black-and-white TVs. ■ Flush with capital, Muntz bought the Kurtis opera-

tion for $200,000. Retaining the basic shape of the car, he made room for a rear seat by stretching the wheelbase to 113 inches. Cadillac's 331-cubic-inch (5.4-liter) overhead-valve V-8, with a bore and stroke of 3.8 inches by 3.6 and an output of 160 hp, became standard power, producing a top speed of 110 mph and a 0-to-60 mph time of 8 seconds flat. Renamed the Muntz Jet and sporting the "Madman" symbol on the horn button, the revamped car stood ready for sale in 1950. ■ After building twenty-eight Jets in his Glendale plant, Muntz moved the operation to Evanston, Illinois, where he cut costs through improved production methods. The wheelbase was stretched again, to 116 inches, the aluminum body changed to steel, a choice of Lincoln power added, and the original Hydra-matic augmented by a three-speed manual with Borg-Warner overdrive. ■ Muntz's clever advertising brought customers, but in spite of the $5200 price he lost $1000 per car and abandoned the project in 1954. Production estimates vary between 200 and 400. Later, with the arrival of color TV, the Muntz empire suffered another setback. Frank Kurtis, on the other hand, became the Fifties' most successful builder of Indianapolis racers. ■ Today, the Collection's Glendale-built Muntz stands as a rare reminder of an effort that, in spite of its maverick spirit, paved the way for the American sports car.

ALFA ROMEO

TIPO 6C 2500S BERLINETTA

■ When a car that represents the pinnacle of both a manufacturer and a coachbuilder also plays a role in world events, it assures for itself an important place in automotive history. The Collection's Alfa Romeo is such a car. ■ Società Anonima Lombarda Fabbrica Automobili—Alfa for short—was formed in Milan in 1910. An improved version of the firm's first car entered the 1911 Targa Florio, establishing Alfa's racing credentials right from the start. ■ After World War I, Nicola Romeo's investment in the firm added his name to the badge and initiated a steady flow of fabulous machines. The Vittorio Jano-designed 6C 1500 and its successors confirmed the greatness of the marque, compiling countless racing victories. ■ Concurrent with its sports cars, Alfa Romeo also built Grand Prix racers. The P2 captured the 1925 World Championship for Manufacturers, adding a laurel wreath to the Alfa badge. The subsequent P3 won every Grand Prix of the 1932 season—one of the most impressive feats in racing history. In the late Thirties came the culmination of the road Alfas, the fabulous 8C 2900—the fastest production car of its day. Also emerging at this high point was the 6C 2500. ■ The "two-five's" exquisite powerplant was a straight six, sporting double overhead cams and hemispherical combustion chambers. Bore and stroke were 72 mm by 100, displacement 2.5 liters (150 cubic inches) and output 95 hp at 4600

rpm, for a top speed of 100 mph. Suspension was independent all around, brakes were four-wheel drums and transmission four-speed non-synchromesh. The advanced chassis, with its 118-inch wheelbase, formed a worthy foundation for a dramatic body created by Carrozzeria Touring. ■ Beginning in 1926, Felice Bianchi Anderloni and his Touring firm made their mark with its classic clothing for sports cars in general, Alfas in particular. Starting in 1937, the firm augmented coachbuilding technology with its patented "Superleggera" or "superlight" system that replaced traditional wood body framing with a light tubular steel skeleton covered by a thin aluminum skin. ■ The collection's Alfa—one of 66 S-versions built, of which half were fitted with the Touring body—was a gift from Mussolini to his mistress Clara Petacci. As the Allied forces in Italy tied an ever-tightening knot around the dictator, he and his mistress decided to make a dash for the Swiss border, using the Alfa for the escape. Not far from their destination, however, they were apprehended and executed. ■ The Alfa spent some time impounded by the local police before an American soldier brought it to the U.S. Today, its history verified by Petacci's wartime bodyguard, this survivor stands resurrected by the Collection's own restoration shop—a symbol of automotive design at its best and a memento of a tragic chapter in history.

N A S H

AMBASSADOR CUSTOM

■ The fortunes of Nash were shaped by three men, all masters in the game of survival. Abandoned by his parents at the age of six, Charles Nash learned to fend for himself the hard way. By the time he was thirty-one, he had risen to the vice-presidency of Durant-Dort; at forty-eight, he was president of General Motors. ■ A falling out with Billy Durant led to Nash's buying the Jeffrey Company in 1916. The following year saw the Nash badge for the first time, affixed to virtually unchanged Jeffreys. ■ Nash introduced his first eight-cylinder car in 1929, managing a $7.6 million profit in a Depression-ravaged 1930. By 1933 the bad times had caught up, however, and only 15,000 were sold, causing a loss of $1.2 million. By the mid-Thirties, Nash had regained its momentum—in 1936, sales zoomed to 53,000 and kept soaring. ■ With all indicators on the rise, Nash began searching for a successor. His choice fell on George Mason, president of Kelvinator. Mason was interested—but only if he could take the refrigerator manufacturer with him. Nash assented, and in 1937, Nash and Kelvinator became a strange but viable alliance, and Nash retired to his Beverly Hills mansion. ■ As a boy, George Mason picked mustard for fifty cents a week. As a young man, he sold cars for fifty dollars a month. An engineering degree landed him jobs with Studebaker and Dodge. After a stint in banking, he returned to cars, now with

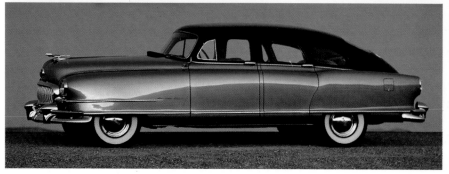

Maxwell and Chrysler, before taking over at Kelvinator. ■ As the head of the independent Nash, Mason knew he needed products with a distinctive look. The answer, the Airflyte series, was introduced in 1948, the year Charlie Nash died. Inspired by a wartime model sculpted by Ted Pietsch and Holden Koto, some thought the Airflyte resembled a spaceship, others a bath tub. Among their innovations was a body featuring advanced unit construction as well as reclining front seats. Nash said the seats were for sleeping, but an awakening teenage population soon saw other possibilities. For whatever reason, the two cars that made up the series—the 600 and the Ambassador—sold like hotcakes. Nash production peaked at 190,000 units in 1949, generating a tidy profit of $26 million. ■ In 1951, the Ambassador Custom Sedan, priced at $2501, received a new grille. Power came from an overhead-valve six, with a bore and stroke of 3.4 inches by 4.4 inches, a displacement of 235 cubic inches (3.8 liters) and an output of 112 hp at 3400 rpm. Weight was 3445 pounds, wheelbase 121 inches. ■ In 1954, it was Mason's turn to bite the final bullet, and George Romney, his handpicked successor, took over. Romney, who had learned the business by putting on overalls and getting his hands dirty, led Nash into the merger with Hudson, which would ultimately create the foundation of American Motors.

PACKARD

MODEL 1708 TOURING CABRIOLET

■ Nineteen thirty-nine was a watershed year for Packard. Not only did the company celebrate its fortieth anniversary—although with scarcely a mention, except by the press—but the year also marked the end of the magnificent Twelve, the last of the Senior Packards. Also that year, the company began producing its twelve-cylinder PT boat engine for the Navy—an ominous sign of the dark period to come. ■ The most outstanding of the classic Packards—the V-12-powered Ninth to Seventeenth Series—had been introduced in 1932 as the Packard Twin Six, although its designation was changed to Packard Twelve the following year. ■ Work on the V-12 powerplant had commenced in 1930, when Cornelius Van Ranst, a brilliant engineer of Cord L-29 fame, was hired by Packard on a contract basis. Van Ranst's brief had actually called for him to develop a front-wheel-drive V-12 chassis, but by the time a prototype—which eventually ran at speeds of 110 mph on the Packard proving grounds—had been completed, management had opted for a conventional layout. ■ In its original configuration, the Van Ranst V-12, a 67-degree, modified-L-head design, featured a bore and stroke of 3.4 inches by 3.5, a displacement of 375 cubic inches (6.1 liters) and an output of 150 hp at 3500 rpm. For a multi-cylinder engine, it was a small package, originally intended to power a new mid-size line of Packards. Instead, this

PACKARD SERVED THE POLICE AS WELL AS THE POSH

marvel of smoothness, duly increased in displacement, was mated to one of the most sophisticated Packards ever built. ■ By the time it reached production as the 1932 Twin Six, the Packard V-12 had had its bore and stroke increased to 3.4 inches by 4.0, which resulted in a displacement of 446 cubic inches (7.3 liters) and an output of 160 hp at 3200 rpm. The specifications were changed again in 1935 with the introduction of the Twelfth Series to 3.4 inches by 4.3, 473 cubic inches (7.8 liters) and 175 hp at 3200 rpm. ■ For 1939, the year of the Collection's choice—a Brunn-built, 139-inch wheelbase Touring Cabriolet weighing some 5845 pounds and priced at $8355—the Twelve's basic specifications remained unchanged: three-speed transmission with vacuum-controlled free-wheeling; vacuum-boosted, twin-shoe Bendix brakes; pressed-steel frame with X-shaped center brace channels; and independent front suspension. ■ During the last year of production, just 280 V-12s were built, of which less than a dozen were bodied by Brunn. These top-of-the-line Packards were favorites of numerous world leaders; the Collection's example, armor-plated to resist 50-caliber machine gun bullets, was used by a succession of Mexican Presidents. Still wearing appropriate seals and flags, this impressive survivor remains unrestored, a magnificent reminder of the last great Packard.

MERCEDES-BENZ

300SL COUPE

■ In the early Fifties, after the paralysis of the war years, Mercedes-Benz began to yearn for the glory of the past, an era when the supercharged roar of its racing giants sent shock waves of awe across Europe's Grand Prix circuits. The decision to return to racing was more than sentimental, it was logical. What better way to generate interest in a new line of production cars? ■ It fell to veteran engineer Rudolph Uhlenhaut to prepare a car for the great return—no simple task, as he was forced to work with an existing engine, a tall, single-overhead-cam straight-six, designed for the firm's luxury line. Bore and stroke were nearly square, 85 mm by 88, creating a displacement of 3.0 liters (183 cubic inches). Ready to race, it generated 175 hp at 5200 rpm. ■ Uhlenhaut solved the need for a low hood profile by placing the engine at a 45-degree angle. But not only was the engine tall, it was also heavy, requiring Uhlenhaut to come up with an ultralight skeleton. Again, he drew on his talent for the unorthodox, creating a space frame built from a network of small-diameter steel tubes. In order to preserve structural strength, however, the design could not accommodate conventional doors. The solution? Roof-hinged "gullwing" doors. ■ The 300SL—the S standing for Sport, the L for Leicht, meaning light—was first put to the test in the 1952 Mille Miglia, where it lost to a Ferrari. But from then on, the 300SL

produced a straight flush, winning the Swiss Grand Prix, Le Mans, the German Grand Prix, and finally, the most grueling of them all, La Carrera Panamericana. ■ The story might have ended there, had it not been for the vision of Max Hoffman, New York's super-purveyor of sports cars. He convinced Mercedes to build a road version of the 300SL, backing his enthusiasm with an order for 1000 examples. ■ Uhlenhaut—complemented by Walter Häcker on the styling side—went back to the drawing board. The basics of the racer were kept intact, including its tubular frame and upward-opening doors. The engine also remained, but was fitted with fuel-injection—a first for a gasoline-fueled production engine. This, along with a new cylinder head, upped performance to 240 hp at 4800 rpm. Although civilization increased the 300SL's weight from 1918 pounds to 2700, its top speed was an impressive 140 mph plus—enough to make the 300SL the fastest car of its day. ■ Despite a price that soared to nearly $10,000, Mercedes lost money on the project. After building 146 cars in 1954, 867 in 1955, 311 in 1956, and 76 in 1957, for a total of 1400, the Gullwing—as it was unofficially called—was replaced by a less exciting roadster. ■ Just one step from the race track, the 300SL—a blend of the primitive and the refined—is one of the most striking interpretations of the sports car ideal.

MERCEDES-BENZ

TYP 770K OFFENER TOURENWAGEN

As the Third Reich and its megalomaniacal leadership marched inexorably towards its apocalyptic climax, the might of its muscle—as far as automotive preference was concerned—was manifested by the Grosser Mercedes, produced in two generations from 1930 to 1943. ■ The unforgettable images of imperious party dignitaries plying the oceans of mass hysteria in their conveyances of steel and rubber made the Grosser Mercedes an inseparable part of the lore of the Third Reich. Yet the deplorable elements of this dark era were certainly not the inanimate objects, but rather their diabolical occupants. ■ First shown at the 1938 Berlin auto show, the second-generation Grosser Mercedes—by then reserved for party dignitaries—was quite different from its 1930-38 predecessor of the same name. Referred to by Daimler-Benz as the W 150, the 770K sported a completely new chassis with independent suspension both front and rear. ■ Power still came from the 7.7 liter straight eight—its black-lacquer exterior subtly complemented by chrome accessories and engine-turned alloy surfaces—with its bore and stroke of 95 mm by 135. Thanks to increased compression, however, the output now reached a supercharged maximum of 230 hp at 3200 rpm. The transmission remained unchanged except for the addition of a fifth gear. ■ The Grosser Mercedes—"gross" meaning big in German—would

■ THE 770K WAS THE MOST MASSIVE OF MERCEDES

reach its peak with the W 150. Its wheelbase had grown by 5 inches to 155 inches, the overall length by 16 inches to 240 inches. A handful of vehicles received armor plating, which increased weight by some 2000 pounds. Also part of this package was bullet-proof window glass, as well as special tires whose two dozen separate chambers limited damage when punctured. ■ Some automotive historians suggest that a very few of these armor-plated giants received special treatment under the hood. The added weight certainly called for added power, and more efficient breathing would have been the answer. This was accomplished with four valves per cylinder, two twin-throat carburetors and double superchargers, features that would have upped output to a stunning 400 hp at 3600 rpm—enough to propel the mastodon to speeds in excess of 110 mph. ■ Altogether, 88 units were built —the special vehicles included. The example featured here—a single-supercharger, non-bulletproofed version—was delivered in 1943 to the Führer's personal retreat in Berchtesgaden. The Collection also has on display the only automobile that specifically mentions the Führer's name on its registration documents. ■ Regardless of their sinister application, these automobiles, with their brilliant engineering, compelling proportions and magnificent craftsmanship, represent one of the high points in automotive history.

117

FORD

THUNDERBIRD

■ Compared to its European counterpart, the American sports car was always an elusive breed. Before World War I, the most sporting cars were the roadsters and runabouts from makers such as Mercer, Stutz and Simplex, whose rarity resulted as much from the deplorable state of the roads as from any other reason. ■ Between the wars, suggestions of the American sports car could be seen in several rakish speedsters, the Auburn Boattail attaining a stature all its own. After World War II, the European definition of a sports car—a racing machine more or less civilized for road use—gradually gained a foothold in America, inspiring such efforts as the Crosley Hot Shot and the Kurtis 500K. ■ In the eyes of the public, however, it was not until the introduction of the Chevrolet Corvette that the American sports car finally arrived. Although it still expressed more style than substance, it set a trend that its rivals would have to follow. ■ Ford had harbored plans for a sports car since 1951, but as soon as the Corvette appeared, everything was moved to the front burner. The Thunderbird was not to be a sports car in the true sense, however. Although it possessed the elements of a track-bred weekend racer—two seats, sporty styling and good performance—it became a small, luxuriously appointed automobile that helped Ford define "the Personal Car." ■ Judged on its styling, the Thunderbird was one of the cleanest

designs of the era, the work of a team headed by Bob Maguire. And in terms of performance, Ford's Personal Car again proved to be on target; unlike the Corvette, it had V-8 power right from the start. ■ By the end of 1956, some 32,000 cars had been built, but for 1957, the Thunderbird would receive a styling revision in the spirit of the Fifties, with fins and a longer rear deck. Also available was a porthole-enhanced hardtop, a design destined to become a favorite of the smart set. ■ The example chosen for the Collection—pretty in Colonial White and Starmist Blue—sports the second most powerful of four engine options available that year. The overhead-valve V-8—its breathing capacity improved by twin four-barrel Holleys—has a bore and stroke of 3.8 inches by 3.4 and a displacement of 312 cubic inches (5.1 liters). Output is 270 hp at 4800 rpm, top speed around 110 mph. The 102-inch wheelbase package weighs 3134 pounds and features a three-speed manual transmission. Its original sticker carried a base price of $3408. ■ By 1958, the Thunderbird had become a different animal, growing additional seats and gaining 500 pounds. Although the Corvette would eventually fulfill the ambitions of the American sports car enthusiast, the 53,166 copies of the original Thunderbird created a large following—admirers whose love and loyalty proves that Ford was on the right track.

CHRYSLER

IMPERIAL PARADE PHAETON

■ Few occasions lend so much prestige to a vehicle as its majestic descent amid lines of cheering crowds. We think of the flickering images of ticker-tape parades honoring returning heros, the classic hoods and fenders of Marmons and Cadillacs littered with the barometer of Wall Street gone wild. ■ In the early Fifties all this weighed heavily on the shoulders of the men whose responsibility it was to keep Chrysler before the eyes of the people. From General Manager K. T. Keller down the line to the public relations office, it was agreed that putting Chryslers on parade was good publicity. ■ In 1951, Chrysler began building three vehicles for precisely that purpose. These would be headquartered strategically around the country—in New York, Detroit and Los Angeles—and be made available to dignitaries on a request basis. ■ The project was assigned to Chrysler stylist Virgil Exner and his staff—mostly his staff, because Exner was in the midst of a major revamp of the Chrysler lines. Inspiration was taken from the 1941 Newport show cars and their dual-cowl configuration. The chassis were Crown Imperial limousine units, with wheelbases stretched to 147.5 inches, creating an overall length of 241 inches. Stock 1951 Imperial grilles and front and rear bumpers were used to assure identity with the showroom line, but everything in between was all-new. ■ The West Coast car made its debut at the 1953 Tournament of

Roses parade in Pasadena, carrying Grand Marshal and Vice President-elect Richard Nixon. Other dignitaries who revealed themselves to the masses from the seats of the Chrysler ranged from Churchill to Khrushchev. ■ In 1955, the cars were returned to Chrysler for updating. This time, 1956 Crown Imperial front-end sheet metal, including grilles, bumpers, hoods and fenders were mated to the appropriate parts from the rear, including Imperial fenders complete with gun sight tail lights. ■ Power for the 5814-pound behemoths came from Chrysler's overhead-valve V-8 hemi, with a bore and stroke of 3.8 inches by 3.6, a displacement of 331 cubic inches (5.4 liters) and an output of 250 hp at 4600 rpm. Each car used a two-speed Powerflite automatic transmission. ■ Duly revitalized, the cars returned to their respective locations. After years of service, the Los Angeles car was sold to the City of Los Angeles, in whose hands it still remains. The Detroit car was vandalized and had to be scrapped. The New York car saw extensive use in State Department and White House service, on numerous occasions carrying President Eisenhower. In 1964, it was returned to Chrysler and was subsequently acquired by the Collection. Still in its original condition, the magnificent Eisenhower car recalls a time when both automobiles and ceremonial pomp were celebrated on a grand scale.

CADILLAC

SERIES 62 CONVERTIBLE

■ After the drudgery of war, the arrival of peace sent Americans on a binge of self-indulgence. With money to spend and a continent to discover, the automobile emerged as the national symbol of freedom and prosperity. ■ Prodded by an appetite that bordered on the insatiable, the limits of taste were continuously tested; the consumer turned from pupil to tutor, and the Fifties became automotive styling's era of excess. ■ The man uniquely equipped to define and exploit these urges was Harley Earl. It seems no coincidence that he was born in Hollywood, the capital of dream imagery. After appropriate schooling, Earl took charge of his father's custom shop, where he built cars for the stars. The mechanisms that would bring on the birth of the Dream Machine were in place. ■ Earl came to Detroit at the urging of Cadillac chief Larry Fisher, whose 1927 LaSalle became Earl's first showcase as well as a harbinger of the type of automobile that established its status primarily on visual appeal. ■ By the end of the war, most luxury automobiles had succumbed to the Crash and its legacy of despair. True, Packard had survived, but its decline had started before the war and could not be stopped. This left Cadillac to emerge as the reigning heir to the luxury car throne. ■ Three decades after Earl arrived at Cadillac, he continued to consolidate its position as a style leader. His 1949 Le Sabre showcar introduced an array of air-

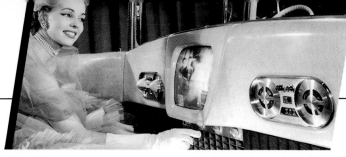

■ A DREAM MOTIF THAT NEVER MATERIALIZED

craft-inspired elements, and soon all cars sported bomb sights, bullets and sweep spears. ■ In 1949, Cadillac became the first mass-produced car to incorporate tail fins. The following year, Earl's creed of Lower and Longer brought even greater excitement to the Cadillac line. By 1953, the Eldorado defined a new direction, incorporating a wraparound windshield for the first time on a production car. In 1957, the Eldorado Brougham introduced quad headlights—another first. ■ The standard Cadillac line for 1957 was stylish enough, as illustrated by the Collection's Series 62 Convertible, delectably finished in metallic pink. Exactly 9000 were built, each carrying a sticker price of $5225. Power came from Cadillac's potent 365-cubic-inch (6.0-liter), overhead-valve V-8, with a bore and stroke of 4.0 inches by 3.6 and an output of 300 hp at 4800 rpm. The body, 216 inches long, languished atop a 130-inch wheelbase. Hydra-Matic drive, power steering and power brakes were standard on all Cadillacs. ■ In 1959, General Motors announced Harley Earl's retirement. As he prepared to leave, the 1959 Eldorado Biarritz Convertible—the epitome of Cadillac Fifties styling—arrived on the scene. Featuring Detroit's most outrageous fins ever, conspicuously accented by dual bullet-shaped taillights, the Eldorado was a fitting monument to a man who would be remembered as Detroit's dream maker.

PEGASO

TIPO Z-102 B

■ To be truly "exotic," a car must be supremely fast, display brilliant engineering, be produced in limited numbers, sport futuristic styling and demand an astronomic price—all characteristics embodied by the Pegaso. ■ This jewel among exotics—its badge animated by the winged horse Pegasus—was the progeny of Spaniard Wifredo Ricart. After founding his own industrial engine firm in Barcelona in 1920, Ricart joined Alfa Romeo as a technical advisor in 1936, later overseeing the construction of the Tipo 512, 162 and 163 racing projects. None would ever see action, however, a fact Enzo Ferrari, whose Scuderia severed its ties with Alfa during Ricart's tenure, never failed to point out. ■ In 1945, Ricart joined the newly created Spanish concern Empresa Nacional de Autocamiones, which was to manufacture trucks in the former Hispano-Suiza factory in Barcelona. ■ The decision to build a sports car was justified on the grounds that it would be both a showcase for the firm's technical acumen as well as provide training for its apprentices. With profit not a prime motivation, a cost-no-object attitude resulted in a product of supreme quality. ■ If there were ever any doubts as to Ricart's genius, the unveiling of the first Pegaso, the Z-102, at the 1951 Paris Salon effectively dispelled such notions. Although the car could claim no direct racing lineage, its design reflected a competition concept of the purest

and most advanced form. ■ Power came from a 90-degree aluminum-block V-8, in one of three displacements—2.5, 2.8 and 3.1 liters, each sporting four overhead cams. Bore and stroke of the 2.8-liter version was 80 mm by 70, which, with four Weber carburetors, produced 170 hp at 6300 rpm. Performance proved shattering: In 1953, a flying-mile record attempt resulted in a new mark of just under 150 mph. ■ Chassiswise, the specifications were also stirring—as if lifted from the blueprints of a Grand Prix car. Suspension was all-independent; for ultimate balance the five-speed gearbox had been engineered in suite with the rear axle and was joined by inboard drum brakes. There was no frame as such, as Ricart had developed an advanced monocoque design utilizing a short, 102-inch wheelbase. Weight was a mere 2160 pounds. ■ The factory offered standard body styles, but these were conservative compared to the avant-garde designs created for Pegaso by Carrozzeria Touring of Milan. The Collection's example sports a body by Saoutchik, whose restrained effort belied the typical flamboyance of the Parisian coachbuilder. ■ Pegaso had entered the sports car arena without fanfare, relying on its merits for exposure. When, in 1958, it was time to exit, this exotic among exotics did so without drama—Ricart simply retired, leaving some 100 magnificent machines by which we may judge his genius.

EDSEL

PACER CONVERTIBLE

In a historical sense, spectacular failure may sometimes appear as conspicuous as spectacular success. Epics like Napoleon's march on Moscow come to mind. As far as failure in the automotive arena, nothing can compare with that of the Edsel. ■ The overt part of the story began in August of 1956 with Ford's announcement that a coast-to-coast network of dealers for a brand-new make was to be established. From then on the public was inundated with news of the Edsel, one bit of information more startling than the other, such as the fact that over $250 million was being spent on its development…or that first-year sales could be expected to surpass an incredible 200,000 units. ■ When the 1958 Edsels were finally introduced in September of 1957—early, so as to give them a jump on the competition—it was an anti-climax of pathetic proportions. In addition to the fact that car prices in general had escalated dramatically—and buyers therefore stayed away from dealerships—the Edsel's styling was a disappointment. Regarded as grossly overdone, outrageous and tasteless, it was, in a word, vulgar. ■ The first-year Edsel lineup consisted of five models. Two of them, the Pacer and the Citation, were offered as convertibles. The example depicted on these pages, a Pacer, was reproduced only 1876 times. Based on the 1957 Ford Fairlane 500, the wheelbase was 118 inches, weight

4311 pounds. Power came from the Edsel-exclusive "E400" overhead-valve V-8, breathing through a single four-barrel carburetor and featuring a bore and stroke of 4.0 inches by 3.5, a displacement of 361 cubic inches (5.9 liters) and an output of 303 hp at 4600 rpm. ■ Base price was $3028, which included self-adjusting brakes and a three-speed manual transmission. In addition, there was an endless list of options, including both overdrive and automatic transmissions. If one wished for something more advanced than a column-mounted shift lever, the "Tele-Touch" featured selector buttons protruding conveniently from the center of the steering wheel hub. ■ From a peak of 20,000 units in August 1957, when optimism was still high, output was cut to less than 2500 units per month in November and December. The total for the model year was a dismal 63,000. ■ For the 1959 model year, in spite of the fact that the advertising people were able to so eloquently put their finger on the spot with the slogan "Edsel—Already an Expression of Good Taste," sales dropped to less than 45,000. The 1960 model year saw the completion of only 2846 cars. ■ In November of 1959, the Edsel was officially killed. There may not have been any epic qualities about its failure, but, in defeat, the Edsel could finally be seen with more forgiving eyes, emerging years later as a modern classic.

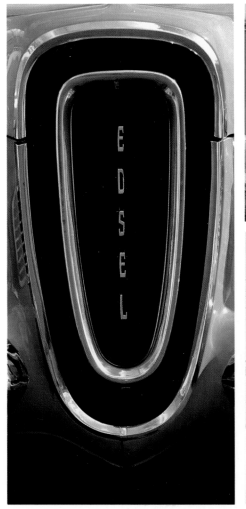